STEPHEN HAWKING

STEPHEN HAWKING

THE THEORETICAL PHYSICIST WHO SHAPED OUR VIEW OF THE COSMOS

CHRIS MCNAB

ACKNOWLEDGMENT

Thanks go to Sten Odenwald for his scientific review and to Lucy Doncaster for her careful editing, although any mistakes remain my own.

This edition published in 2025 by Arcturus Publishing Limited
26/27 Bickels Yard, 151–153 Bermondsey Street,
London SE1 3HA

Copyright © Arcturus Holdings Limited

All rights reserved. No part of this publication may be reproduced, stored in a retrieval system, or transmitted, in any form or by any means, electronic, mechanical, photocopying, recording or otherwise, without prior written permission in accordance with the provisions of the Copyright Act 1956 (as amended). Any person or persons who do any unauthorised act in relation to this publication may be liable to criminal prosecution and civil claims for damages.

AD011082UK

Printed in the UK

CONTENTS

Introduction 7
Chapter 1 Boundary Conditions 11
Chapter 2 Hawking in Context............................31
Chapter 3 Cambridge 63
Chapter 4 Into the Black Hole 87
Chapter 5 No Boundaries 113
Chapter 6 Worms, Strings and Peas 137
Chapter 7 To the Stars 161
Conclusion 191
Bibliography 195
Notes 201
Index..205
Picture credits 208

INTRODUCTION

For those of us who do not work in the domains of theoretical and experimental physics or cosmology – yes, that's almost all of us – the number of scientists we can list off the top of our heads can be single-digits small. We would start with the two most obvious candidates, drummed into us from our schooldays and from popular awareness – Sir Isaac Newton and Albert Einstein. From there, the next most famous candidates might be Galileo Galilei, Nicolaus Copernicus and Johannes Kepler, perhaps even Michael Faraday and James Clerk Maxwell. After that, unless we are scientifically interested or have had a scientific education, we might start to run out of steam, but for one further name: Stephen Hawking.

Stephen Hawking died in 2018. In life, he was a theoretical physicist of the highest order. His prolific output of work literally changed our understanding of the universe. His most famous outputs explored the origins of the universe, especially what we call 'Big Bang theory', and the nature of black holes. Hawking's work in these areas alone would constitute the life's work of many physicists. But his inexhaustible appetite for sheer hard work, married with his compulsion to go ever deeper into the theoretical and mathematical universe, led him into many different domains of physics. He made seminal contributions to our thinking about the nature of space and time (or 'spacetime'), the size and shape of the universe, our relationship to reality, the possibilities of multiple universes, the theoretical viability of time travel, and much more.

Exceptional and important academic output does not, in itself, create a high profile with the general public. There are legions of

INTRODUCTION

supremely influential scientists, men and women who have pushed the envelope of knowledge over the last, say, 50 years, who remain well below the radar of most people. (To illustrate, a survey commissioned by Research!America in January 2021 found that 72 per cent of the Americans polled could not name a single living scientist.[1]) Hawking, by contrast, became a genuine household name. He did so by punching through the barrier between academics and the general public, offering high-level scientific answers to the greatest human questions in language that almost everyone, with some effort, could understand. He democratized theoretical physics and cosmology and it made him a bona fide celebrity, a status that he embraced.

But the climbing brilliance of his mind was inverse to the irresistible decline of his physical body. Hawking was visibly and profoundly disabled by motor neurone disease. While his mind soared to the outer reaches of the universe, to the beginning of time itself, his adult body reached a point at which he could not walk, talk, move, feed himself, wash himself, and even breathe for himself. Even blinking one eye became a strain. As least part of the reason for his exceptional success was that his personal story was as heroic as his scientific journey. Hawking himself was candid about this truth: 'To my wider colleagues, I'm just another physicist, but to the wider public I became possibly the best-known scientist in the world. This is partly because scientists, apart from Einstein, are not widely known rock stars, and partly because I fit the stereotype of a disabled genius.'[2]

In this book, the physical struggles faced by Stephen Hawking, and the impact those challenges had on his personal and professional life, are undeniably central to the story. Yet we should

INTRODUCTION

never take that focus too far, just as we should not become overly obsessed with some of the celebrity elements of Hawking's life (although to omit the most, and many, colourful incidents would be remiss). Stephen Hawking was, first and foremost, a brilliant scientist. Without that foundation, he would have remained largely anonymous to the wider world. He was driven by his thirst to discover what physicists call a 'Theory of Everything': a complete, unified explanation of how the universe works, from its most majestic expressions (including the universe itself) down to the behaviour of indivisible subatomic particles. Such a theory was, for Hawking, not an abstract dream but a vigorously pursued intellectual quest, one that he came, arguably, close to resolving.

In this biography, it is essential that I endeavour to explain some of the major theories Hawking advanced. Many caveats are required here. First, Hawking's scientific research and personal journey are naturally intertwined, but for thematic clarity I will switch my focus between one or the other, rather than attempt an unswerving chronological narrative. The time gap between the two narratives, however, will be kept to a minimum. Also, Hawking was a world-class theoretical physicist; this author is not. Much of Hawking's work in the mathematically dense academic papers is impenetrable to most apart from theoretical physicists. Thankfully, Hawking himself wrote explanatory works for people just like us, and it is from those that I draw my information. Nevertheless, even Hawking's popular works are challenging, so I have also utilized a range of supporting sources, many of which are listed in the Bibliography. Beyond my efforts, however, I would recommend that the reader takes the slow, mindful time to read some of Hawking's works directly. I recommend one or all of *A

INTRODUCTION

Brief History of Time, *The Universe in a Nutshell*, *The Grand Design* and *Brief Answers to the Big Questions*. If this book simply whets the appetite to read Hawking in his original voice, I will have succeeded here.

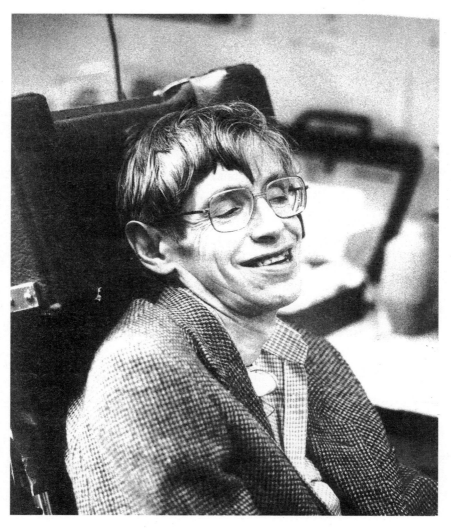

A relaxed photograph of Stephen Hawking, taken in the early 1990s.

CHAPTER 1
BOUNDARY CONDITIONS

Academic greatness is not something lightly achieved. Intellectual wattage is only part of the equation, albeit an important one. Added to the equation are many other factors. Personality is key, having the steadiness of mind to pursue ideas and to defend them in a public realm, although academia is often more accommodating of eccentricity of character than many other professions. Money is also critical; how many superbly bright people are there in the world who didn't go to university simply because they couldn't afford to, or because financial demands took them in other directions? This takes us to what is probably the most important factor of all: opportunity. Unless a developing young mind is given the meaningful chance to pursue education, in the right places at the right time, all the brilliance in the world might fade from view. In the case of Stephen William Hawking, his parents ensured he had the opportunity. Now he only had to seize it.

FIRST STEPS

Both Hawking's parents, Frank and Isobel, were academics by vocation. But unlike many university-educated individuals of their era, they had not come from money. This made a big difference in an age when higher education was often either bought or won.

Frank Hawking's background lay in Yorkshire agriculture. In the past, his family had attained both status and prosperity through farming, but in the early 20th century their wealth dribbled away through the fingers of Frank's grandfather (Stephen's great-grandfather), who was unable to handle overextended debt during a period of economic depression. His son Robert (Stephen's grandfather) tried to prop up the failing enterprise, but instead ran headlong into bankruptcy. Fortuitously, Robert's wife, Mary (neé Atkinson), the daughter of a cabinetmaker, had a small family property in Boroughbridge, North Yorkshire, which was turned into a school. Fees from teaching not only provided a financial lifeline but were also sufficient to send their son, Frank, to university.

And not just any university. Frank studied medical science at Oxford University, which was, and remains, one of the world's most prestigious centres of learning. He was a bright, successful student, winning scholarships and prizes to compensate for the lack of family money, even managing to send some remuneration home in support. Frank received his BA with first-class honours in 1927 and, following clinical research at St Bartholomew's Hospital (Barts) in London, his Doctor of Medicine (DM) in 1933.

Frank had a nose for adventure, an instinct that his son would later share. A specialization in tropical medicine took him on a 1937 research expedition to East Africa. When war broke out two years later, he made an arduous and perilous overland trek across the African continent before working his way back to the UK, intent on joining the armed services and fighting for his country. The authorities told him he was far more valuable in his role in medical research, so there he stayed.

Stephen's mother, Isobel Eileen Hawking (née Walker), was Scottish, one of a family of eight children. Born in Dunfermline, she spent much of her childhood in Glasgow, where her father was a local doctor. When she was 12, the Walkers headed south to

BOUNDARY CONDITIONS

England, settling in Devon. Supporting the large family on a doctor's salary meant money was tight. But like Frank's parents, Isobel's parents placed a high value on education and made financial sacrifices to support their bright daughter's application to Oxford.

University was a rare path to take for girls at the time. The first award of degrees for women at Oxford only occurred on 14 October 1920 (Cambridge held out longer, following suit only in 1948). Few women had the opportunity, encouragement or finances to attend university anyway. By 1930, only about 20 per cent of UK university students were women. But Isobel was one of the exceptional few. She studied a combined course of Philosophy, Politics and Economics at St Anne's College.

Following the completion of her degree, Isobel's jobs included working as an Inspector of Taxes for the Inland Revenue, a job she disliked intensely. She replicated Frank's yearning for adventure; she even attempted to participate on the Republican side in the Spanish Civil War in the late 1930s. Politically, the Hawking family leaned towards the left; indeed, Isobel had even been a member of the Young Communist League – the youth section of the Communist Party of Britain – before the Second World War broke out in 1939. Her resolute trip to Spain was short-lived, however; she was sent back to the UK when she didn't quite meet the requirements of front-line life. Eventually, she settled into a role as a secretary in a medical research centre, where she met, courted and eventually married Frank Hawking.

Stephen was the first of three children born to Frank and Isobel. He was a wartime baby, born in Oxford on 8 January 1942. Hawking liked to note that this date was exactly 300 years after the death of Galileo (1564–1642), a landmark figure in the history

13

BOUNDARY CONDITIONS

Stephen William Hawking at the tender age of four in 1946.

of physics, astronomy, and general scientific theory. The family at this time actually lived in Highgate in North London, but Isobel retreated from the blitzed capital to bomb-free Oxford to give birth. (Back in Highgate, Frank survived a near strike from a German V-2 ballistic missile.)

Stephen had two sisters. The first, Mary, was born in 1943, and the second, Philippa, in 1946. The family later expanded with the addition of an adopted brother, Edward. In his own short autobiography, *My Brief History*, Hawking described Edward as 'very different from the other three children, being completely non-academic and non-intellectual, which was probably good for us'.[3] A fondness for Edward is evident, as is sadness: Edward died in 2004, most likely from poisonous fumes inhaled during a flat renovation.

'Eccentric' seems to be the term commonly applied to the Hawking family and Stephen's childhood home environment. Both his parents were intellectually curious, and it showed in the clutter of learning. Stimuli surrounded the Hawking children – books lay in scattered piles or were double-stacked on bookcases; gramophone music filled the air (apparently Wagner was a stirring favourite); conversation was continual and lively, freely ranging across subjects, but especially the sciences. Isobel would take the children to the great London museums, often leaving Stephen alone there and picking him up later in the day.

In his autobiography, Stephen sketches some early memories. He remembers crying in considerable distress when his parents first tried to take him to nursery, specifically Byron House School in Highgate. Nursery was therefore promptly skipped, but Hawking would attend Byron House primary school until he was eight.

The Highgate area of London was noted for its intellectual culture, and Byron House was popular among the aspirational parents, offering a progressive model of education in which students led the direction of their studies. Hawking recalled telling his parents he wasn't learning anything. (It should be noted that Stephen admits he didn't really acquire functional reading skills until he was eight, much later than his sisters.) Other eclectic memories included playing on local bomb sites with his friend Howard and the demotivation caused by a low-quality clockwork train set, which fell well short of Stephen's fervent expectations. He subsequently used his own saved money to buy an electric train set, but it also failed to deliver.

In 1950, the circumstances of the Hawking family changed considerably, for the better. Frank Hawking became the head of the Division of Parasitology at the National Institute for Medical Research in Mill Hill, on the north-west edge of London. To shorten the commute, the family moved out to nearby St Albans. They now occupied a sizeable Victorian house, a vast expanse for the children to explore, complete with novelties such as servants' bells. It fostered imaginative games, such as finding innovative new ways to enter the building. The house was not necessarily inviting, however. Frank had a parsimonious relationship with money, especially in relation to his own comfort or personal environment, although ironically Hawking remembered he could be generous to others. This meant that the dilapidated features of the house – and there were many – often went unfixed or were imperfectly repaired by Frank. The house had no central heating (Frank refused on grounds of cost), so during winter the family became strange and hulkish figures, wrapped in excessive layers of clothing in the effort to stay warm.

St Albans had, by Hawking's own perception, a very different social character to that of Highgate. He later described it as 'somewhat stodgy and conservative',[4] qualities that could not be ascribed to the Hawkings. By consequence, the nonconformist Hawking family stood out as something of a curiosity in the neighbourhood. Outsiders who did make it through the front door for dinner reported some strange habits, such as the way that the Hawking family would often sit silently through a meal, each with his or her head bent down into a book. Their mode of transport also didn't help them maintain a low profile; Frank's insistence that they couldn't afford a new car meant that he instead bought a pre-war London black taxi.

Hawking later admitted that his parents made few friends. But internally, the family had an energy all of its own. For holidays, they would take breaks in a genuine gypsy caravan, complete with brightly painted woodwork and heaps of rustic character, which Frank and Isobel had bought and set up in Osmington Mills, on the south coast of England. Ever watching the pennies, Frank converted a cupboard in the caravan into sleeping quarters for the children.

Although Frank did invest time and (restrained) money into his family, he could be a somewhat absent figure as a father, typical of the era in which he lived. The absences were emotional and physical. Hard work absorbed much of his bandwidth. At the Mill Hill Institute, his primary focus was upon 'chemotherapy', which was later rebranded as 'parasitology'. He was a prolific scientific writer and editor, being joint editor on the important 1950 work *The Sulphonamides* and writing or contributing to more than 100 articles relating to tropical diseases and other biomedical topics. He pioneered research into treatment of lymphatic filariasis (LF), classified as a neglected tropical disease (NTD), and also developed the preventative chemotherapy drug diethylcarbamazine (DEC), still widely used today in the treatment of worm infections. He also made breakthrough discoveries in the treatment of tropical diseases such as bilharzia and malaria.

One of the most insightful descriptions of Frank Hawking comes from his short biography on the website of the Royal College of Physicians (he became a fellow of the RCP in 1965): 'Frank Hawking was not a "hail fellow well met" person; a basic shyness was often misjudged as being compounded by a mixture of self-interest and disinterest in others, but this was wrong. He could be, at times, very kind but his shyness prevented him from offering his help in special circumstances.'[5] This description hints at a sensitive, somewhat distant individual. Hawking's memories chime with this portrayal, but with evident love and respect for his father. On 12 December 2017, Hawking gave a keynote address in Cambridge for Sightsavers, an organization dedicated to fighting global diseases that cause blindness. Hawking anchored the address on his father's work (he noted that his father, like Sightsavers, studied the disease lymphatic filariasis), and gives an intimate insight into Frank's life and legacy, but also his character:

BOUNDARY CONDITIONS

> My father was very hardworking and dedicated to his research. [...] He worked in sometimes very difficult, even daunting, conditions. But he never gave up, and he believed fully in the role of science, to build a better world. He believed in humanity, and our ability to find solutions to the pressing problems he witnessed. But he was modest, and never able to promote himself, which meant that he was not really recognized for his contribution during his lifetime. I often feel my father deserves his own biography. His was a fascinating and remarkable life.[6]

In this quotation, Hawking is taking note of how character can affect a scientific career, especially in relation to *publicly acknowledged* success. As we shall see, regardless of the physical condition affecting his outer frame, Stephen Hawking was no wallflower when it came to driving his ideas in the public domain. For the son of the father, scientific work needed to be watered by *visibility* if it were to grow and – to give it a utilitarian frame – to have the greatest amount of influence on the greatest number of people.

Frank Hawking's character may have been somewhat inaccessible, but there is no doubt that Hawking regarded him as formative on his outlook. Frank was certainly invested in his eldest son's scientific education. He often took Stephen to his place of work at the laboratory at Mill Hill, where Stephen remembered squinting through microscopes at specimens and wandering through the tropical insect houses. Frank also gave his young son some tuition in mathematics, albeit only to the point where Stephen's own mathematical abilities exceeded those of his father. It is safe to say that the investment Frank Hawking made in his son's scientific development paid a healthy return with interest.

Once the family was settled in St Albans, Hawking's formal education continued. The first school he attended there was, incongruously, the St Albans High School for Girls, the name of the school belying the fact that it accepted boys until the age of ten. The young Stephen certainly seemed intellectually capable and evidently smart, but his preference leaned more towards self-education rather than classroom learning. Accounts of his school years reveal an ability to absorb and process information and ideas rapidly, meaning that the steady pace of a formal curriculum could rather bore him. St Albans High School for Girls did bring a significant encounter, at least in retrospect. Also at the school was one Jane Wilde, two years younger than Stephen. She would, many years later, become Stephen's wife, although they did not communicate at the school. She just remembered a boy with 'floppy-golden-brown-hair'.[7]

One month into Stephen's schooling at St Albans, Frank set off for Africa again, this time on an extended research trip. During his absence, Isobel received, and accepted, an offer for her and the children to go and stay on the Balearic island of Majorca, in a villa at Deià on the north-west coast. The invitation was extended by Beryl Graves, an old university friend of Isobel and also the wife (since 1949) of Robert Graves, the renowned English poet and writer. It seems to have been an idyllic time, four months under Mediterranean warmth. For Stephen, formal education did not cease entirely during this time. He attended the same tutoring sessions as Robert's son, William. The tutor was apparently distracted in his duties and the instruction largely consisted of giving the boys passages of the Bible to read and essays to write in response. However casual this method, it did give Stephen a good grounding in Scripture, which in the future would help him to wrestle with questions that embraced both science and spirituality.

Eventually, the time came to return to England. Once home, Stephen took the important 11-plus exam. Introduced in 1944, the 11-plus was an examination administered by some schools in England, Wales and Northern Ireland to determine which type of secondary school a child would attend. Those who achieved high marks could progress to more academically prestigious 'grammar schools' or private schools. (Note also that in the UK at this time, what were known as 'public schools' were actually fee-paying private schools.) 'Primary' education took the child to the age of 11, 'secondary' education took them onwards to 16.

Stephen passed the exam comfortably and began attending St Albans School, a prestigious institution founded in 1309, but with roots in a monastic school dating back to 948. He would spend the whole of his secondary education in St Albans School, despite his father's failed effort to place him in the renowned Westminster public school when his son was 13 years old. In his autobiography, Hawking reflected on how his father was burdened by a sense of class inferiority and saw access to the best schools as a means for his son to find a place at the top table of society. Stephen was ill on the day of the scholarship exams, however, and the family couldn't afford the fees without that scholarship. Nevertheless, looking back, Hawking felt that continuing his education at St Albans School was to his benefit rather than detriment.

As Stephen Hawking transitioned from child to teenager, we start to see the first signs of the brilliance that would characterize the man. He was quick-witted and knowledgeable for a young person, so much so that he acquired the nickname 'Einstein' among his peers. Some remembered that he had a slight edge of arrogance about him, although this was evidently not severe enough to prevent him from forging a strong friendship group. His intellectual powers, however, were compromised by a tendency to drift into laziness, at least when it came to his formal schooling. He dropped down from the top academic stream to settle somewhere in the middle.

Regardless of his school performance, the teenage Stephen Hawking was driven by curiosity. His leaning was towards scientific and mathematical subjects, although not to the exclusion of other intellectual domains. By his own admission he was 'always very interested in how things operated, and I used to take them apart to see how they worked'.[8] He appeared fascinated by *systems*, and the connection between the theoretical and experimental domains, although at his age he likely wouldn't have expressed it in those terms. With his friends, he invented various board games with fiendishly complex rules. They included a game that involved mapping out labyrinthine family trees, and one called 'Risk' that required corporate, logistical and financial decision-making of such demand that a single game could extend over several days.[9]

Other practical pastimes included making model aircraft and boats. And computing. Famously, in 1958 Stephen and his friends actually built a working computer called the 'Logical Uniselector Computing Engine' (LUCE). Stephen's previous electronic projects had included converting a TV into an amplifier (resulting in a serious electric shock) and making his own record player. The more ambitious LUCE was constructed from a wide array of electronic and analogue parts, including a telephone switchboard. According to a rather demotivating article in the school newspaper, *The Albanian*, 'The machine answers some useless, though quite complex, logical problems.'[10] The modified version, however, was able to make simple mathematical calculations successfully.

It was also at this stage that a serious interest in cosmological physics took hold. Hawking remembered being shocked at the age of 15 when he heard that scientific theory and tested evidence concluded that the universe was in a state of expansion, which to him had the logical implication that the universe was becoming ever emptier. He also had earnest conversations among his friends about the origins of the universe, not least whether an act of divine fiat was required to start the ball rolling. He was intrigued by the verified theory that universal expansion, or inflation, could be deduced by the fact that the light from far-off galaxies was at the red end of the light spectrum, while closer galaxies leaned towards the blue end of the spectrum. To his young mind, the idea of a universe in endless growth was something of an affront: 'An essentially unchanging and everlasting universe seemed so much more natural.'[11] He likely had little inkling that these early interests would in many ways turn into the foundation of his entire career.

OXFORD

As Stephen entered his final two years of secondary education, he decided to narrow his focus more on mathematics and physics. (English children of the ages 16–18 who didn't go into work would take 'A-levels' (they still do) in school or college as the entrance qualifications for university.) Stephen's passion for mathematics had been stirred by Dikran Tahta, one of St Albans School's more passionate teachers. Tahta was a man whose whole career was dedicated to mathematical education, his receptive audience ranging from school pupils like Stephen to university students.

While Tahta and Stephen might have thrived on mathematics, Frank was rather cool about his son's pursuit of the subject; he saw few future job prospects via a mathematical specialism. He had rather hoped that Stephen would follow his father's academic route in biology and medicine. Accepting that was a step too far, Frank instead sought to redirect his son's interest towards chemistry. Stephen did indeed have an abiding interest in chemistry, not least because it provided ample opportunities to make strange concoctions or even produce chemical explosions.

Where Frank and Stephen were united was that both had their sights set on University College, Oxford. Founded in the 13th century, and thereby Oxford University's oldest institution, University College was Frank's alma mater. Stephen looked to go there to read physics and chemistry, which were taught under the banner of 'natural science'. Being the child of a college alumnus could certainly help oil the wheels of admission, but the fact remained that Stephen needed to win his place in the college through good results in his A-levels and a university entrance exam.

The headmaster of St Albans School was sceptical about Stephen's chances. The young Hawking was certainly bright, but he was also young; he would be attempting to take the entrance exam and enter Oxford at age 17, whereas the other two St Albans School boys taking the exam were a year older, with the additional education and confidence that brought with it. Furthermore, there was some disruption in Stephen's life at this time. His mother, father and siblings, drawn by Frank's work, had left the UK for India for a full year, settling in Lucknow in Uttar Pradesh province in the far north of the country. Stephen was not entirely cut off from his family during this time: he went to stay in India during the months of the summer school holidays. This trip implanted vivid, quirky memories: his father's committed British refusal to eat any 'foreign' food; getting stuck in their car (which Frank had actually shipped from England) as monsoon waters rose around their wheels, requiring a tow to safety; renting a houseboat that they sailed around the extraordinary tropical beauty of Lake Kashmir. For the rest of the year, Stephen lived with Frank's research colleague, Dr John Humphrey, where he was able to keep on top of this important year of schooling.

Whatever he did, it paid off. Stephen achieved exceptional scores in his entrance exam, well above the requirements. He also aced the in-person interview with university admissions staff. Thus he was accepted into University College to study natural sciences. Hawking has since noted that beyond his education at St Albans School, his subsequent career brought no further formal education in mathematics; he was essentially self-taught in the subject from the age of 17 onwards. For someone who would later use mathematics to unpack the secrets of the universe, that is a laudable achievement in itself.

We might imagine that after Hawking joined Oxford University in October 1959, he straightaway plunged headlong into long hours of diligent study, inspired by both his subject and the brilliance of the people around him. The reality is more underwhelming. As Hawking would later explain, the academic culture of Oxford during the late 1950s separated students into two basic categories. There were those students who had such natural soaring brilliance that for extremely little effort they could walk away at the end with a first-class degree. Then there was the mass everyone else, intelligent students who would also apply themselves minimally, accepting the fact that they would leave with a far lower class of degree. Apparently, the idea of working hard to get the best possible degree was regarded as unseemly. Indeed, Hawking described the Oxford culture as 'very anti-work'.[12] This attitude was not helped by the fact that there were no exams to be taken until the very end of a three-year degree. Hawking once calculated that his total volume of study over three years came to about 1,000 hours, or roughly one hour per day.

Oxford's rich social life also didn't come easily to Hawking. At the age of just 17, he was younger than most of the students around him, often considerably so. Many of the other male students had also done two years of national service in the armed forces, and were worldly and mature. For the first two years at Oxford, therefore, Hawking found it hard to mix with others, and he became lonely and isolated.

All that changed in the third year of study, by which time he had a few more years of development under his belt. He joined Oxford's illustrious Boat Club, famed for fielding the university team that rows the pathologically competitive annual Oxford and Cambridge Boat Race. Although the wiry and slight Hawking did not have the brawn to participate as a rower, he did find a position as a coxswain (colloquially referred to as the 'cox'), who took responsibility for steering the slender boats and guiding the rhythm of the eight-man rowing crew. By his own admission, Hawking was not a natural cox, on several occasions unerringly guiding the boat into collisions or other minor calamities. But more important, he was accepted by the club as one of its own, indeed became highly popular. With a mischievous streak, and an evident enthusiasm for alcohol-fuelled social events, Hawking merged into the group's social energy, and was all the happier as a result.

BOUNDARY CONDITIONS

During a lecture given in 2016, Hawking shares a light-hearted photograph from his days in the Oxford Boat Club; he is centre-front, in the boater hat.

There remained, of course, the matter of his academic work. An additional problem for Hawking was that he found much of the coursework boring, exceeded by the pace of his own learning and his ability to hoover up knowledge and ideas. Hawking tended to downplay his intellectual performance at Oxford, but others around him clearly remember an emergent distinction. A fellow physics student, Derek Powney, later recalled that he, Hawking and two other physics undergraduates received a 13-question assignment on the subject of electricity and magnetism. They were given a week in which they should tackle as many of the questions as they could, presenting their conclusions in the next tutorial class. The day of the tutorial came around and the students compared notes. Aside from Hawking, none of the students had managed to complete more than one and a half of the questions, such was their challenge. Hawking himself had gone the extra mile in the opposite direction and completed no questions whatsoever. Feeling the pressure, Hawking skipped all his morning lectures (the tutorial was in the afternoon) and set out to do as much as he could. When the students reconvened after lunch, Hawking had managed to complete *ten* of the questions. It was then that the other students realized Hawking might be operating on a different level.

The final Oxford examinations eventually arrived at the end of three years of indifferent study and (latterly) exuberant socializing. Hawking had done little in the way of preparation and revision, and spent the night before the first exam in a state of sleepless turmoil. What revision he had done had concentrated on acquiring theories rather than the time-consuming accumulation of facts. There was much riding on these exams. By this stage, Hawking had already set his mind on post-graduate doctoral work at Cambridge, which had a global reputation as a centre of excellence and experimental innovation in physics. For that next step, Hawking needed to secure a first-class degree.

Poor sleep and inadequate preparation were counterbalanced by his exceptional mind, but his final grade was on the hesitant borders between a first-class and a second-class degree. To determine his final grade, he faced a viva voce (an oral examination) with his examiners. He met the questioning with evident bravado. In reply to one of the questions about his future plans, he replied: 'If I get a First, I shall go to Cambridge. If I receive a Second, I will remain at Oxford. So I expect you to give me a First.'[13] The entertaining logic of the reply helped tilt the examiners in the desired direction. Hawking received his first-class degree and so was destined for Cambridge.

Between Oxford and Cambridge, Hawking decided to spread his wings with a semi-educational foreign holiday, assisted by a university travel grant. Accompanied for the first leg of the trip by a Farsi-speaking student, John Elder, Hawking travelled to Iran. Given the limited international air travel available in those days, the outward journey involved long, snaking train rides across Europe, the Balkans and into the Middle East. The first major destination was Tehran, the Iranian capital. From there, Hawking teamed up with another student and went deeper into the country, exploring some of the great historical sites of Persian history. But when Hawking finally set his sights for home, the adventure took a downward turn. He became quite seriously ill with dysentery, which made enduring a bone-shaking bus ride across the country even more unpleasant. As the bus passed through Buin Zahra, Qazvin province, a devastating magnitude 7.1 earthquake struck

BOUNDARY CONDITIONS

on 1 September 1962, Buin Zahra being the epicentre. Hawking did not remember this event, partly from the delirium of his illness, partly because the general dramatic lurches of the bus masked seismic effects. Nevertheless, at some point Hawking broke a rib as he was thrown into the seat in front of him. He actually only found out about the earthquake several days after it had occurred; more than 12,000 people had died in the disaster. Upon reaching Istanbul after many long, uncomfortable days of travel, Hawking finally sent a postcard to his anxious parents telling them that he was all right; they hadn't heard from him in ten days, and all they knew from his last communication was that he was travelling through the earthquake zone.

Set on a postage stamp, a wistful portrait of a teenage Stephen Hawking, before he felt the full effects of his disease.

Having endured, survived and recovered from his Iranian experience, Hawking could now look forward to his future at Cambridge. But there was something else, insidious and occasional, that was also attracting his attention. In his final year at Oxford, Hawking had begun to notice some curious disruptions in his sense of balance and co-ordination. The dexterity needed to scull a boat on Oxford's rivers became a struggle. He noted that he seemed to be getting clumsier, occasionally falling over for no good reason. In one instance, he took a nasty tumble down a flight of stairs, hitting his head and experiencing a temporary loss of memory.

BOUNDARY CONDITIONS

Something was happening deep within Hawking's body. For now, the excitement of youth, life and the future could override the concerns. But not for long.

CHAPTER 2
HAWKING IN CONTEXT

In October 1962, Stephen Hawking headed to the University of Cambridge to begin his programme of doctoral research. Ahead of him were four of the most consequential years of his life. The events that would occur within those years forever changed what Hawking might refer to as his personal 'arrow of time'. First, they would establish Hawking's ground-floor credentials as an exceptional and ambitious physicist, particularly in his chosen domain of cosmology; by the end of his doctorate, the world of physics

In the early 1960s at Cambridge, Hawking began to use a cane to assist walking, although his condition seemed to stabilize in the first two years after diagnosis.

was sitting up and paying attention to his theories. Second, and in challenging counterbalance to the first thread, over his four years at Cambridge Hawking's health would undergo a profound and irreversible decline. The concerning symptoms that first emerged at Oxford would magnify terribly at Cambridge, leading to a diagnosis and an illness that would forever change the direction of his life. How Hawking encountered and faced the early years of his physical deterioration are the subject of the next chapter. In this chapter, by contrast, we need to do some intellectual scene-setting.

Academic theories are almost never conceived in an intellectual vacuum. They are usually either a proof, critique or extension of a body of existing ideas, even when the new theory is of groundbreaking import. It is impossible, therefore, to go forward and understand Hawking's work without giving some insight into the state of play in physics in the early 1960s. And what an exciting time it was. Hawking entered Cambridge at a moment in which theoretical and experimental physics were making revelatory new interactions, driven by advances in both mathematical constructs and in powerful new observational and computational technologies. The work and laws that constituted 500 years of 'classical' physics – the output of luminaries such as Galileo, Newton, Kepler, Laplace, Faraday, Maxwell and others – had, in the first half of the 20th century, been challenged and in some cases overturned by a new generation of exceptional thinkers, including Planck, Einstein, Heisenberg, Schrödinger, Fermi, Dirac and Bohr. Seen through their eyes, everything from atoms and light to time and space were radically revised. The world would never look the same again.

Hawking's work at Cambridge and beyond advanced both classical and modern physics. Here we will outline the critical body of work on which Hawking built his new ideas. In doing so we can also take advantage of the fact that Hawking devoted much of his working life to explaining essential physics to a popular audience, most famously in *A Brief History of Time* but also in a much wider body of books, articles, interviews and other output. Therefore, in this chapter I will take the opportunity to explain some of Hawking's own illuminating descriptions of the physics that he either embraced or overturned. Note that a full and detailed explanation of all foundational work in physics by 1962 would be impossible here. Consequently, I will just focus upon those theories that had the most bearing on Hawking's future research.

CLASSICAL PHYSICS

While much of what we call classical physics was challenged in the first half of the 20th century, its salient laws and theories still hold true in most cases when applied to our observable universe. Classical physics gave us the fundamental understanding of how objects move, how gravitational attraction works, how sound and light propagate, how heat and energy are transferred, the role of disorder, the relationship between electricity and magnetism, and many more fundamental propositions about how matter and forces interact. There are various ways to slice the cake of classical physics, but in terms of relative importance to Hawking's work we can focus on three core sub-categories: classical mechanics, classical electrodynamics and classical thermodynamics.

Newtonian physics

As I have mentioned, no physicist is an island, but Sir Isaac Newton (1642–1727) – the father of classical mechanics – certainly comes close, and would be a solid contender for the title of greatest physicist of all time. Hawking noted with some undisguised pride that the esteemed academic position of Lucasian Chair of Mathematics, officially founded for Cambridge University by King Charles II in 1664, was held by both him and Newton, albeit three centuries apart. In *A Brief History of Time*, Hawking refers to Newton's 1687 publication *Philosophiæ Naturalis Principia Mathematica* (Mathematical Principles of Natural Philosophy) – generally abbreviated to the *Principia* – as 'probably the most important single work ever published in the physical sciences'.[14] Most enduringly, the *Principia* explained the three fundamental physical laws that govern the interactions between objects and the forces acting upon those objects (at least in terms of interactions well below the speed of light). These were:

1 An object will remain in a state of rest, or in motion at a constant speed on a straight line, unless it is acted upon by a force.
2 The force acting upon an object is proportional to its mass multiplied by its acceleration, and is made in the direction of the straight line in which the force is applied. (It was this Second Law that gave the equation $F = ma$, where F is Force, m is mass and a is acceleration.)
3 To every action, there is also an opposed and equal reaction; the forces have the same magnitude, but take opposite directions.

These three laws have, collectively and individually, stood the test of time. Almost anything that moves or collides with another object, for any reason, is governed by these laws, hence they are applied in numerous practical domains that demand calculated determinations, from engineering to sport. And almost every theory within physics, however abstruse, will typically connect with or reference Newtonian physics at some point. For example, in Hawking's later work the notion of Newtonian relativity would be important, derived from the First Law. In this important framing of mechanics, an object at rest or one moving at a constant velocity (the speed of something in a given direction) are referred to as inertial frames of reference, within which the Newtonian laws act equally. A common example of how this works could be to imagine two people, one standing stationary on a train platform and the other on a train moving at a constant velocity through the station. Each has a ball in their hand, and even though they are in different states of motion, if they throw the ball directly upwards it will fall straight back down into their hand. This applies even on the moving train; the train itself is an inertial frame of reference. This is important because it means that we cannot speak of a single defining inertial frame of reference. The motion of an object is not absolute, but relative to a chosen reference frame; to the man on the train, he is the one who is stationary and the man on the station is the one who is moving, for example.

In the *Principia*, Newton also outlined his law of gravitation, which was related to his Third Law and extended earlier ideas about gravitational attraction, such as those advanced by Galileo's experiments with falling and rolling objects and Johannes Kepler's theories of planetary motion. Hawking noted that the story of Newton conceiving his gravitational law after an apple fell on his head is a quaint invention, but through his law he demonstrated the physical principles of elliptical planetary orbits. Newton provided an accurate mathematical framework of how objects large and small were all governed by a universal force of mutual attraction. The fundamental equation of the law stated that any two bodies are attracted to one another by a force that is directly proportional to the product of their masses (i.e. the bigger the objects get, the greater the attraction) and inversely proportional to the square of the distance between their centres. Hawking always understood that many of his readers did not have a solid mathematical understanding, so in his books and essays he provided a helpful clarification, explaining that if the distance between two objects is doubled then the gravitational force between them is divided by four, and if the distance triples the force is divided by nine, and so on.

What was especially important about Newton's force of gravity was its 'universal' attraction: it applies equally to an apple resting on a lawn as it does to our Earth orbiting the Sun. Cosmological clarifications related to planetary orbits were particularly revelatory. Newton showed that a smaller orbiting body was essentially falling towards the larger body it orbited, but that it maintained enough forward velocity perpendicular to the gravitational pull to keep it from actually spiralling into and striking its dominant partner. Essentially, an orbiting body is forever falling but never arriving.

In *A Brief History of Time*, Hawking briefly expanded on an important cosmological problem within Newton's law of gravitation. The question was this: if planetary bodies are attracted to one another by gravity, wouldn't that imply that the stars and planets would move towards each other over time, eventually all meeting at a single point? Newton's historical counter to this was that if there were an infinite number of stars distributed over an infinite space (as opposed to a finite number of stars in a finite space), then the absence of a single gravitational focal point would prevent the collapse. Later in this book, we will explore how Hawking reflected on the possibility of the 'Big Crunch', the ultimate contraction of the universe in on itself (the opposite of the original 'Big Bang'). But in *Brief History*, Hawking observes that in an infinite universe every point in that universe is in effect a centre and also notes intriguingly that, 'We now know it is impossible to have an infinite static model of the universe in which gravity is always attractive.'[15] Newton's limitation was that, unlike Hawking, he didn't have a theoretical model of a universe that is in a state of expansion or contraction.

Electrodynamics

Imagining the branches of classical physics as the legs of a three-legged stool, another of those legs is classical electrodynamics. The contributors to this domain are many, but its most significant figures are André-Marie Ampère (1775–1836), Michael Faraday (1791–1867) and particularly James Clerk Maxwell (1831–79). Both Ampère and Faraday explored the symbiotic relationship between electricity and magnetism, but it was Maxwell who detailed that these were actually two sides of the same coin. He therefore unified electricity and magnetism into a single theory, in which he showed how oscillating electric and magnetic fields travel through space at a constant speed as electromagnetic waves. Maxwell's calculations revealed that constant speed was that of the speed of light, and that light itself was an electromagnetic wave.

In *Brief History*, Hawking devoted some time and reflection to Maxwell's theories, especially the concept of 'wavelength', a wave-like disturbance in the electromagnetic field. Hawking asked the reader to imagine that these waves were like ripples emanating out across a pond. The wavelength of the ripples could be regarded as the distance from the crest of one wave to the crest of the others next to it. In electromagnetic forces, the wavelength determines the type of electromagnetic radiation involved, with different wavelengths corresponding to different parts of the 'electromagnetic spectrum'. Thus, wavelengths of more than 1m (3ft) are classified as radio waves, while wavelengths of just a few centimetres in length are microwave energy. Infrared radiation, by contrast, has a wavelength of 700 nanometres (nm; 1 nm = 1 billionth of a metre) and visible light is in the 400nm to 700nm range. At the even smaller end of the wavelength scale, we find ultraviolet light, X-rays and gamma rays.

Maxwell gave to the world a model of electromagnetic force that had a profound impact on both theoretical physics and practical electrical engineering. But as Hawking explains in *Brief History*, Maxwell and some contemporaries tripped up significantly in how they understood the movement of electromagnetic waves across space. In the same way that sound waves move through the medium of air, Maxwell and other influential figures posited that in the realm of empty space, light moved at a constant speed through a nebulous stationary medium exotically called the 'luminiferous aether' (shortened to 'aether' or 'ether'). Hawking explained that the implication of this was that: 'Different observers, moving relative to the ether, would see light coming towards them at different speeds, but light's speed relative to the ether would remain fixed.'[16] In 1887, however, this theory was dealt a hefty blow by the scientists Albert Michelson (1852–1931) and

Edward Morley (1838–1923), at the Case School of Applied Science in Cleveland. Through a brilliantly devised optical experiment, involving a device called an 'interferometer', Michelson and Morley compared the speed of light in the direction of Earth's travel through space – i.e. directly through the posited aether – to its speed at a right angle to Earth's motion. The prediction was that if the aether existed, light would actually move faster in the direction of Earth's motion and slower in the perpendicular direction. They found no difference in the two speeds, however. The Michelson–Morley experiment was one of the most significant experiments of the 19th century, and although the concept of the aether would struggle on it would be dealt its final blows in the 20th century by none other than Albert Einstein.

Thermodynamics

We now turn to thermodynamics, the branch of physics that focuses on the relationship between heat, energy and work. Study in this field before the 20th century led to what are known as the 'four laws of thermodynamics'. Here we shall briefly outline the first two of those laws, as they would be central to Hawking's later work on black holes. The first law is also known as the 'law of conservation of energy'. Simply expressed, it means that the energy within a closed system cannot be created or destroyed, but is rather converted from one form to another. This might initially sound counter-intuitive, as don't we experience the disappearance of energy all the time, such as when we turn off a light or when someone dies? But this law demonstrates that energy lost in one form is simply moved to another form. For example, when the driver of a moving car applies the brakes to slow the vehicle down, the kinetic energy of forward motion is not lost but rather converted into heat energy as the friction heat generated in the brake discs. This heat energy then, in turn, is dissipated into the surrounding air and ground. If we regard the car, brakes, ground and air as the closed system, we see that no energy is either lost or created.

The second law deals with a fundamental property of the universe called 'entropy'. Entropy is effectively the measure of disorder or randomness in a system. With rather gloomy portent for us, the law states that again in a closed system – and we can regard the universe as such a system – entropy always increases. Imagine this in terms of a sandcastle on a beach. Leave the sandcastle exposed to the elements, and it will always turn back into unstructured sand particles. What we don't see are millions of sand particles spontaneously arranging themselves into beautifully crafted sandcastles. It takes human hands to build the sandcastle, but this temporary pushback against entropy (i.e. the human creating localized order) comes at the loss of heat energy within the muscles of the sandcastle builder, which in itself is part of the long-term entropic process for human beings. Furthermore, when two entropic systems are combined the resultant entropy is greater than the sum of the individual entropies found in the original systems.

In *Brief History*, Hawking explains entropy in terms of an imaginary box that features a gas-tight internal partition. The left-hand side of the box is full of gas molecules, all energetically bouncing off the walls in which they are confined. If the partition is removed, the gas spreads out to fill both halves of the box – the entropy has increased, as the molecules are now in a more disordered state. Hawking points out that the second law of thermodynamics isn't infinitely prescriptive. It *is* possible that even with the partition removed the gas molecules could collect themselves neatly on one side of the box; it is just massively unlikely.

Entropy was a theoretical construct that would play a foundational role in Hawking's ideas. But Hawking also shows convincingly that entropy is absolutely central to our experience of the 'arrow of time', our inveterate sense of forward motion from the past to the present to the future. This is why if we run a movie backwards, however smoothly, we can always tell that it is backward movement, because we sense the flouting of entropic reality. Hawking puts this in terms of a cup on a table – the cup can go from an ordered state (intact on the table) to a disordered state (smashed on the floor), but never in the opposite direction. Hawking argues that the arrow of time not only consists of the thermodynamic and psychological arrows working in tandem, but also with the cosmological arrow of time created by an expanding universe. But more on that later.

Entropy is central to so much of Hawking's thinking. He would apply the theory not only to detailed physical discussions of the properties of black holes, but also to more philosophical topics such as religion and the boundary conditions of the universe (the constraints or states of the universe at given points in time). Hawking could use both classical physics and modern physics to challenge the sense of who we are, why we are here and where we are heading.

SPECIAL AND GENERAL RELATIVITY

When we move into the 20th century, we quickly begin to witness the widening theoretical fault lines between classical physics and the emerging 'new' physics. At the leading edge of this movement was none other than Albert Einstein (1879–1955).

Hawking noted, with a clear sense of regret, that he never had the chance to meet Einstein in person; Einstein died when Hawking was just 13 years old. Much of Hawking's academic career was essentially a dialogue between himself and Einstein's towering theories, special relativity and general relativity, as transformative in the history of scientific comprehension as Newton's laws. Hawking acknowledged the debt, especially in the way that he and physicist Roger Penrose would apply general relativity to show that 'the universe must have a beginning, and, possibly, an end'.[17]

Hawking also had a fundamental respect for Einstein's big-picture approach to science. In his short profile of Einstein in the Appendices of *Brief History*, Hawking provides a quotation from Einstein to explain why Einstein declined the offered presidency of Israel in 1952: 'Equations are more important to me, because politics is for the present, but an equation is something for eternity.'[18] But Hawking was not absolute in his deference to Einstein's theories. Quantum mechanics (see below) put Hawking at odds with significant parts of Einstein's theories. But without Einstein, Hawking's theories on singularities, the Big Bang, black holes, time and general cosmology had few initial footholds. In *A Brief History of Time*, Hawking provides an overview of both special relativity and general relativity. True to the original theories, these passages form some of the most challenging in an already difficult book.

Special relativity

The year 1905 was crucial for the 26-year-old Albert Einstein, then famously working not in a prestigious university, but rather as a clerk at the Swiss patent office in Bern. In his spare time, Einstein utilized the theoretical models produced by German physicist Max Planck (1858–1947) to argue that light is transmitted in individual 'packets' of energy called 'light quanta', now known as 'photons'. The existence of photons was experimentally confirmed in the 1920s by Arthur H. Compton (1892–1962), through his work on X-ray scattering, and by Robert Millikan (1868–1953), via his confirmation of the photoelectric effect (the emission of electrons from a material, caused by electromagnetic radiation), both of which provided strong evidence for the particle nature of light. In 1905 Einstein published his seminal paper 'On the Electrodynamics of Moving Bodies'. In this landmark work, he challenged our intuitive relationship to time and produced what became known as his 'theory of special relativity'.

The first convincing efforts to measure the speed of light came from Danish astronomer Ole Roemer (1644–1710) in the 17th century, but it wasn't until the second half of the 20th century that light's speed was accurately set at 300,000 km/h (186,000 mph). While Einstein did not have the conclusive experimental data related to light's speed, he convincingly argued that the speed of light was a fixed constant in relation to any inertial frame of reference, independent of the motion of the light source. This theory might sound innocuous, but it has time-distorting implications. Through mathematical proofs and thought experiments, Einstein demonstrated how time – previously considered as an absolute constant (i.e. your clock will agree with my clock) – was itself relative to the observer, at least at light speed or approaching that speed. Hawking explained it thus. In the Newtonian model of time, if you sent a pulse of light from one location to another, the observers of that event would agree on the time the journey took but not on how far the light travelled. This is because time is regarded as an absolute, but space is not. Under this theory, Hawking explains, the speed of light is calculated by dividing the distance it has travelled by the time taken for it to do so, which means that different observers would measure different speeds of light. Under Einstein's theory of relativity, however, all observers must agree on how fast light travels. 'They still, however, do not agree on the distance the light has travelled, so they must therefore now also disagree over the time it has taken. [...] In other words, the theory of relativity puts an end to the idea of absolute time.'[19]

Here is where physics entered the domain of philosophy. The constant speed of light meant that time itself was relative to observers. This was not just a matter of perception, but one of *reality* – time is *actually* relative, a phenomenon known as the 'relativity of simultaneity'. The faster you travel, the slower time runs, a truth proven experimentally in high-altitude aircraft experiments. Synchronize two atomic clocks, and place one on a fixed location on the ground and another on an aircraft. Fly the aircraft at high altitude around the world and when it gets back to the position of the ground clock the airborne clock will be slightly, ever so slightly, at an earlier time than its partner.

The relativity of time means that whenever we locate an event in the three dimensions – e.g. within a co-ordinates system of length, width and height – we should also consider the time of the event as the fourth dimension in the co-ordinates. As Hawking says: 'In relativity, there is no real distinction between the space and time coordinates, just as there is no real difference between any two space coordinates.'[20]

Hawking also spotted a problem in special relativity, one that both affects Newtonian physics and was a productive complication for Einstein. Hawking explained that in the Newtonian theory of gravity, the gravitational effects between two bodies are instant in time. Under this framework, for example, if the Sun in one second suddenly leapt a million miles from its current position, the Earth would *instantly* respond to the change in the force of gravity between the planet and its star. But if that were true, this would imply that there were something that could travel faster than the speed of light, as light typically takes about eight minutes to travel from the Sun to the Earth.

One of the other great leaps taken by Einstein in 1905 was to demonstrate that *nothing* could travel faster than the speed of light. In this equation, T is the observer's time, tp is the traveller's time, v is the relative speed between them and c is the speed of light.

$$T = \frac{tp}{\sqrt{1 - (v/c)^2}}$$

If the relative speed is greater than c, the square root becomes an imaginary number... a sign that real events are limited by the speed of light. An identical formula exists for the increase in mass with speed.

As Hawking clarifies in *Brief History*, because speed adds to mass, any speed beyond light speed would be impossible because not only would it require infinite energy to reach that speed, but the mass of the object would also become infinite as it reached the condition of $v = c$ in the process. Einstein's work was no mere paper idea, but would have a deep and lasting impact on the world around us – the discovery of the equivalence of mass and energy at an atomic level, for example, provided a theoretical foundation for the development of all-too-real atomic weaponry.

GENERAL RELATIVITY

Einstein next turned his attention to the particular properties of gravity. Ten years later, in 1915, he would publish a theory that would be just as transformative as special relativity, and which Hawking would negotiate in much of his life's work – general relativity. Special relativity changed our understanding of time. General relativity would change our understanding of space. In a mathematically challenging body of theory, known as the 'field equations', Einstein disturbed the idea, previously held as common sense, that gravity was a force. The alternative model presented by Einstein needs some additional context for understanding; the details of this context were also critical to Hawking's work, so are worth exploring.

In physics, there are four forces operating in the natural universe: gravitational force, electromagnetic force, and the strong and weak nuclear forces. I will outline each shortly, but this is a useful moment to clarify the basic relationship between particles and force. When we hear the word 'particles', we might think of molecules or (depending on our scientific knowledge) the individual building blocks of molecules: atoms. Much of our everyday understanding of atomic structure has been based on what is called the 'Rutherford–Chadwick model', jointly developed by the pioneering physicists Ernest Rutherford (1871–1937) and James Chadwick (1891–1974) in the 1920s and 1930s. In this model, a tiny, dense nucleus composed of a cluster of positively charged protons and negatively charged neutrons interact with negatively charged electrons, the existence of which had been proven earlier by J.J. Thomson (1856–1940). The relationship between the nucleus and electrons was orbital; the electrons were envisaged as orbiting the nucleus at distance, like planets taking paths around a distant central sun. This view still prevails in school science and popular thought, but has been revised profoundly by quantum mechanics.

For a time, the protons and the neutrons were regarded as 'elementary' particles – the smallest possible particles, indivisible. But during the decade in which Hawking began his doctoral study, even smaller subatomic particles were discovered, either directly or through their deducted and observed influence. Protons and neutrons, it turned out, were themselves composed of 'quarks'. Hawking devotes some lengthy attention to the subject of quarks in *Brief History* and elsewhere. Here, suffice to say that quarks belong to a category of particle we now call *fermions*, which in *Brief History* Hawking clarifies as 'matter particles'. Fermions are the particles (e.g. quarks, electrons, protons, neutrons) that form matter itself, everything from planets to pet cats. A key point about fermions is that they cannot occupy the same space or quantum state (again, a topic we will come to) at the same time.

In contrast are *bosons*, which Hawking descriptively labels 'force-carrying particles'. Bosons mediate forces between fermions, and unlike fermions, bosons can occupy the same space or quantum state at the same time. Bosons express themselves through the four essential forces that drive the universe:

1 Electromagnetic force – This force governs the interaction between charged particles in the realm of what

we call electromagnetic radiation. Electromagnetic radiation includes energies such as heat, light, radio waves, microwaves and X-rays. The boson of the electromagnetic force is the photon.

2. **Strong nuclear force** – The strong nuclear force has one job: it binds protons and neutrons together in the nucleus. This force operates only over mind-bogglingly small distances, but it is immensely strong (hence the name). Its carrier particle is the gluon.

3. **Weak nuclear force** – This is the third weakest of the forces, responsible for radioactive decay and certain types of nuclear reaction, including the fusion process found in our own Sun. The carrier particles are the W and Z bosons.

4. **Gravitational force** – As we have already seen, this familiar force establishes the attraction between objects through their mass. Gravitational force has an influence between all objects, regardless of size, but it is actually the weakest of the four forces, although it compensates for this fact by prevailing over vast distances across space. The boson, or 'carrier particle', of the gravitational force is known as the 'graviton'; however no such force-carrying particle for gravity has ever been detected and so, experimentally, gravity is not produced by the same mechanism as the other three.

This broad groundwork done, let us return to general relativity. In 1907, Einstein demonstrated mathematically that the effects of a gravitational field are locally indistinguishable from those of a constant uniform acceleration. Picture it through this analogy. Imagine you are in an intergalactic elevator in the vacuum of space. The elevator has no windows; you have no visual frame of reference. If the elevator then proceeds to go up with a constant uniform acceleration, your body will feel downward pressure against the floor. From your frame of reference, there would be no way you could tell whether the pressure on your body was caused by upward acceleration or downward gravity. Bringing this model back down to Earth, Einstein concluded that even a stationary observer on Earth was not in an inertial reference frame, but rather in a state of downward acceleration. This was called the 'principle of equivalence'.

Extending his ideas about gravity further, in 1915 Einstein presented gravity not as a force as classically understood, but rather as the curvature of spacetime caused by mass and energy. (The concept and term 'spacetime' was actually introduced by the German mathematician Hermann Minkowski in 1908, when he described space and time as a four-dimensional continuum.) In effect, spacetime is warped by the presence of large bodies such as planets, stars and black holes. What we might conventionally describe as the pull of gravity towards or around a large body is in fact, according to Einstein, caused by the curvature of spacetime.

The usual, albeit imperfect, analogy for the gravitational effects on spacetime involves imagining a taut rubber sheet on which is drawn a standard co-ordinates grid. This represents our traditional view of spacetime. The lines of the grid are our paths of travel in straight lines between points A and B. Now imagine placing a heavy metal ball in the middle of the sheet. This ball, which represents a large body, sinks down at the place of contact and warps the sheet, distorting the gridlines around it. We could then travel along a specific gridline between A and B, but around the ball itself that gridline and our path of travel would be bent towards the large body, even though we ourselves are still travelling in a straight direction. Einstein showed that the bending of spacetime *was* what we regarded as the force of gravity. Gravity was actually the result of objects following curved paths (what he called 'geodesics') in the curved spacetime around the Earth's mass.

Einstein's general relativity also redefined the relationship between gravity and time. In the theory, time itself is distorted by mass and energy, running more slowly in stronger gravitational fields. For example, imagine Person A was on a supermassive Planet X and Person B was on a Moon-sized Planet Y. Both persons are holding clocks. From the perspective of a distant observer at a fixed point in empty space, Person A's clock would tick more slowly than that of Person B. Over what the observer perceives as the same period, Person A might age only a year while Person B ages 20 years, due to the intense gravitational field of Planet X.

Although general relativity had its initial resisters, it steadily knocked down its objectors and became one of the most categorical theories of our universe. Moreover, despite its seemingly logic-defying implications, it was steadily proven experimentally during the 20th century. In 1919, for example, the British astrophysicist Arthur Eddington (1882–1944) conducted an optical experiment while observing a total solar eclipse from Príncipe, an island off the west coast of Africa, while another team observed the same eclipse from Sobral, Brazil. The experiment demonstrated conclusively that light from the Hyades star cluster was bent by the gravitational distortion of the Sun (this effect is also known as 'gravitational lensing').

General relativity formed a framework for much of Hawking's research. Einstein's set of ten related equations, the field equations, posed a mathematical challenge of the highest order, but for those who wanted to study advanced cosmology, general relativity could not be avoided.

QUANTUM MECHANICS

To understand the big picture of the universe, you need general relativity. But what about the opposite extreme, the atomic and subatomic reality? At the moment Hawking arrived at Cambridge, that domain had also undergone a revolution in thinking. For this was the age of quantum theory, and particularly of its influential branch known as 'quantum mechanics', which concentrated its thinkers on the motion and interaction of particles at the quantum level.

If undergraduate students think general relativity is difficult to understand, the encounter with quantum mechanics can be even more confounding. Hawking realized that the mathematical and much of the theoretical content of quantum mechanics was well beyond the reach of the general public. But he believed that even this arcane branch of science could be made understandable in plain English to the broader population, at least in core concepts and important implications. Here I therefore draw upon *Brief History* as well as other Hawking works, such as his essay 'Can we predict the future?' (By way of caution, note that the physicist Richard Feynman suggested that if you think you understand quantum mechanics, you actually don't.)

The background to quantum mechanics was essentially a centuries-old debate about whether light consisted of waves or particles.

Both sides had their august proponents, but by the beginning of the 20th century the balance of opinion had tipped towards the waves. All this began to change in 1900, courtesy of Max Planck, whom we have already encountered on page 43. At that time, he was working on a sinewy issue in physics called the 'black-body problem', which related to the properties of an idealized object (the 'black-body') that could perfectly absorb all the electromagnetic radiation that hit it and which in turn emitted radiation of a specific spectrum based purely on its temperature. As we have seen, Planck theorized, and Einstein later confirmed in the case of photons, that electromagnetic radiation was actually emitted in discrete 'packets' of energy called 'quanta'. Further calculations seemed to indicate that light acted as if it was *both* particles *and* waves, what became known as the 'wave-particle duality'.

This was unsettling to many physicists. How could something be two different things at the same time? Then in the mid-1920s the Austrian physicist Erwin Schrödinger (1887–1961) introduced the idea of the 'wave function' within his development of 'wave mechanics'. In this radical reconceptualization of particle behaviour, the quantum state of a particle is described in terms of a probabilistic wave, the related equation giving us only the probability distribution of a particle at any given time. Around the same time, German theoretical physicist Werner Heisenberg (1901–76) developed an alternative theory known as 'matrix mechanics'. Heisenberg's work led to his formulation of the 'uncertainty principle', a fundamental aspect of quantum mechanics. Heisenberg demonstrated mathematically that it is impossible to know both the exact position *and* the momentum of a particle simultaneously with precision – the more precisely one is known, the less precisely the other can be determined. This limitation is not just due to measurement interference, but is a fundamental property of quantum systems. Quantum theory also posits that a particle can exist in a 'superposition' of all possible positions and states until it is measured. These probabilities are described by what is called the 'wave function'. The wave function tells us the *probability* that we will find a particle in a certain place or with certain momentum. However, the moment we measure the particle's properties (through whatever form of measurement), the wave function 'collapses', and the particle takes on a definite state, with its position *or* momentum (not both) becoming fixed. Outside the act of measurement, it is in effect meaningless to ask what a particle is doing.

This sounds obscure, but hidden in the theory were some big implications for reality. In his last book, *Brief Answers to the Big Questions*, Hawking explained how quantum mechanics critically undermined the theory of scientific determinism driven by the French scientist Pierre-Simon Laplace (1749–1827) in 1814. Laplace argued that an infinitely powerful being, one who knew all the positions of all the particles in the universe at a fixed point in time, would be able to predict the future with 100 per cent accuracy based on the unfolding of physical laws. The uncertainty principle undercut that theory: 'How could one predict the future, when one could not measure accurately both the positions and the speed of particles at the present time?'[21] Hawking also pointed out that Einstein found the uncertainty principle objectionable on many levels, famously declaring that 'God does not play dice!' Hawking would be less than convinced on that score: 'All the evidence points to God being an inveterate gambler, who throws the dice on every occasion.'[22]

COSMOLOGY

Hawking arrived at Cambridge in October 1962. From the range of sub-topics available to him, he chose to focus his attention on cosmology. By his own admission, this choice put him outside the mainstream when it came to physics in the mid-20th century. At that time, Hawking felt that 'cosmology then was hardly recognized as a legitimate field', with some physicists even regarding it as tantamount to a 'pseudoscience'.[23] The more fashionable action in physics was to be found at the atomic and subatomic levels, especially quantum mechanics, rather than the infinite vastness of space. But Hawking was undeterred. Since his early and earnest childhood discussions about the origins of the universe, he had been motivated by the greatest of questions. Now he felt energized by the possibilities of bringing together cosmology and general relativity, a distant frontier with many theoretical obstacles in the way, but one that for Hawking promised ultimate revelations about the universe and, possibly, why we are here.

By the early 1920s, physicists and astronomers were beginning to rise to the theoretical possibilities and mathematical provocations of general relativity. But from a cosmological point of view, there was a problem at the heart of Einstein's model. If all the elements of the universe were under the influence of gravitational attraction, then logically shouldn't the universe actually be contracting, all its stars and planets inexorably drawn together to a single point endless billions of years in the future? This sat at odds with the prevailing idea that the universe was static, unchanging – a model that appealed to the instinctive and often religiously framed idea of eternity.

To square the circle he had created, Einstein introduced a 'cosmological constant' into his equations, which was essentially an anti-gravitational force that counteracted contraction, so everything could stay nicely where it was. The cosmological constant was not Einstein's more secure work, and serious problems within it first emerged in 1922. In that year, Russian physicist and mathematician Alex Friedmann (1888–1925) gave a convincing argument that because the universe effectively looks the same in every direction, even to observers in different parts of the universe, that implied the universe was actually in a state of expansion. (Think of being inside a cake, dotted throughout with currants and raisins, as it is baked. Wherever you are inside the cake the currants and raisins will appear to be travelling away from you.) Two other scientists – the Dutch physicist Willem de Sitter (1872–1934) and Belgian astronomer Georges Lemaître (1894–1966) – also came to the same conclusion around this time.

But the great cosmological leap forward in universal expansion theory came from American astronomer Edwin Hubble (1889–1953). Hubble was not only a brilliant scientist, but he was also one able to capitalize on much-improved modern generations of telescopes and astronomical observation equipment, especially technologies of spectroscopy (those which study the interaction between matter and electromagnetic radiation).

Since the beginning of the 20th century, there had been a lively debate about the size of our Milky Way and the universe beyond. Much of the debate circled around interpretations of 'spiral nebulae', which were seen as ill-defined clouds of light deep in space. Hubble settled large parts of the debate in 1923 when he was working at the Mount Wilson Observatory in California. Through his observations and calculations, he determined that the spiral nebulae were actually other galaxies, millions of light-years from our own. The universe was suddenly bigger, much bigger, than we had previously thought. Then in 1929, Hubble published a seminal paper in which he demonstrated that the further a galaxy was from Earth, the greater its 'redshift' – its light emission towards the redder end of the light spectrum. Back in 1824, the Austrian physicist and mathematician Christian Doppler (1803–53) had set a framework for what we today call the 'Doppler effect'. This specified that the observed frequency of a wave depends on the relative speed of the source and the observer. Most of us are at least experientially familiar with the Doppler effect as expressed in sound; when the source of the sound is moving towards you, the wavelength of the sound is compressed as it gets closer to you, making the pitch of the sound higher. The same principle applies to light. In *Brief History*, Hawking explains that if a star is moving away from us 'the wavelength of the waves we receive will be longer'[24], which means that the light from those stars will be shifted into the red end of the spectrum, while those moving towards us will be moved into the blue end (blue-shifted). Marry up the Doppler effect with Hubble's observations and you are faced with a fact: the universe is expanding.

Many scientists did not like this conclusion. Einstein, to his credit, quickly admitted that he was wrong, later stating that the cosmological constant was his 'greatest blunder'. (Ironically, in the late 1990s and 2000s there was something of a return to the cosmological constant; Einstein might not have been as wrong as he thought.) Others fought a rearguard action with 'steady-state theory', the hypothesis that as galaxies moved apart from each other new galaxies formed in the spaces between, keeping the universe in an overall state of order and predictability.

HAWKING IN CONTEXT

Steady-state theory was progressively demolished in the 1950s and 60s. In its place came an explosive new theory. One of its early pioneers was Lemaître. His proposition was that if you reversed the expansion of the universe, you would eventually arrive at a point when that universe was contained in an extremely dense and hot point, which Lemaître called the 'primeval atom'. It was from this tiny point that all the matter and energy of the universe violently rushed forth at the moment the universe was born. This moment of creation was labelled by the British astronomer Fred Hoyle (1915–2001) as the 'Big Bang'. He intended the term derisively, but it stuck and remains in use to this day.

In 1965, the Big Bang theory was proven accidentally and experimentally via the inadvertent detection of interference signals by the engineers Arno Penzias and Robert Wilson, while working for Bell Telephone Laboratories. The American astronomer and physicist Robert Dicke (1916–97) confirmed the signals as what became known as 'cosmic microwave background radiation (CMBR)', the all-pervasive electromagnetic remnant of the Big Bang. It was the final nail in the coffin of steady-state theory. During the 1960s, the infinitely dense point of universal origin, a place where spacetime was infinitely curved and where the laws of physics broke down, acquired a name: the 'singularity'. It would be Stephen Hawking, alongside others such as Roger Penrose, who would take us further into the mysteries of the singularity.

BLACK HOLES

The developing theories of gravitational attraction in general relativity and concepts of a primordial singularity were relevant to another area of theoretical physics in the first half of the 20th century, that relating to black holes. It was his study of black holes, more than any other cosmological phenomenon, that would first bring Hawking to the world's attention. Given this fact, in *Brief History* Hawking diligently ensures the reader understands how a black hole typically forms, and an outline of that process is a necessity for what follows. (Here we will simplify greatly and focus on the black holes formed by stellar death.)

A star is born when a large volume of gas (mostly hydrogen) collapses in on itself due to gravitational attraction. The gas molecules heat up through increasing frequency of collision with one another, eventually to such an extent that the process of nuclear fusion takes place ('like a controlled hydrogen bomb explosion'[25]), releasing helium and vast amounts of heat. The heat increases the pressure of the gas, which balances out the gravitational force of contraction. The star remains in this stable state for long periods of time, but eventually the fuel that powers the star begins to run out. Hawking points out the paradox that the larger the star (i.e. the more fuel it starts with), the sooner it will deplete itself, because it needs to burn hotter to counteract the star's gravity.

When a star's fuel begins to fail, the internal pressure of the star is not sufficient to counteract the star's own gravitational contraction. This results in a supernova explosion, in which the outer layers of the star are blasted outwards in an explosion, sometimes of light-years in proportion. After the explosion, a super-dense core is left, but if this is beyond 1.4 times the mass of the Sun its gravitational collapse will increase in strength and pace, eventually reaching the point of infinite density – a singularity – that distorts spacetime so profoundly that light cannot escape, so you can't see it. You now have a black hole.

At the time Hawking went to Cambridge, much work remained to be done on understanding the nature and physics of black holes. In *Brief History*, Hawking gives some historical context. Although the descriptor 'black hole' was actually coined in 1969 by the American theoretical physicist John Wheeler (1911–2008), the idea of these strange cosmic phenomena goes back much further. Hawking explains how the Cambridge natural philosopher John Michell (1724–93) took Roemer's fixed speed of light and theorized that there could exist stars of such enormous density and mass that they induced a gravitational field of a magnitude that could even capture light. By their very nature, black holes would be hidden from sight – 'black voids in space', as Hawking describes them.[26]

Other scientists toyed with this idea, but only in the 20th century did black holes start to take mathematical shape. The Indian graduate student Subrahmanyan Chandrasekhar (1910–95) calculated the size a star would need to be to overcome the outward pressure of the exclusion principle to be unable to resist collapse under its own gravity. 'Chandrasekhar calculated that a cold star [any of several types of star that, roughly speaking, emit little heat or light] of more than about one and a half times the mass of the sun [the 1.4 limit described on page 58] would not be able to support itself against its own gravity.'[27] This crossing point is known as the 'Chandrasekhar limit'.

Although the radical nature of his ideas compelled Chandrasekhar to abandon his work on black holes for something less academically risky, others eventually took up the flame. In 1939, arguably history's most famous American physicist – J. Robert Oppenheimer (1904–67) – published a groundbreaking paper with research student Hartland Snyder (1913–62). This paper

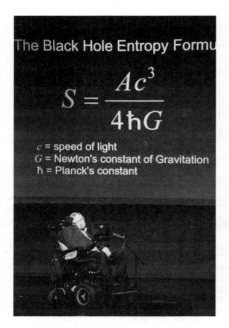

At the STARMUS festival in 2016, Hawking presents his theory of black hole entropy.

essentially provided the mathematical principles for the formation of black holes. Oppenheimer calculated how light cones, 'which indicate the paths followed in space and time by flashes of light emitted from their tips',[28] were bent progressively inwards by the gravitational pull of the contracting star until the pull was so strong that light could not escape outwards to an observer. Nor could anything else, thus the black hole created (by implication) a singularity. Oppenheimer's exceptional and often-neglected research into black holes was then put on hold by the Second World War and his infamous labours on the development of the atomic bomb within the Manhattan Project. But in 1958, American physicist David Finkelstein (1929–2016) defined the 'event horizon' of the black hole, the boundary at which the escape velocity of the collapsed star (the speed needed to escape the gravitational pull) equalled the speed of light. It was rather like the edge of an infinitely powerful whirlpool; once it was crossed, nothing was coming back.

In future years, actual black holes would be detected and observed (to the extent they can be observed directly) by advanced instruments. However, when Hawking began his studies at Cambridge

HAWKING IN CONTEXT

in 1962, black holes were still primarily theoretical objects, known mostly from equations and tentatively implied by their effects on nearby matter. There remained much to be done.

We now have an overarching sense of the scientific context Hawking stepped into as a graduate student. He was embarking on a lifelong intellectual journey into the cosmos. As we shall see, as his own physical body contracted towards immobility, his mind reached ever further and further away from our planet.

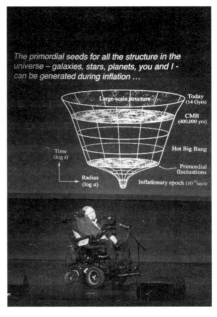

Again at STARMUS, Hawking models the inflationary universe.

CHAPTER 3
CAMBRIDGE

Hawking's excitement to begin his post-graduate studies at Cambridge came with some initial disappointment. Hawking wanted to study under the august British astronomer Fred Hoyle, the Plumian Professor of Astronomy and Experimental Philosophy in Cambridge University. Hoyle was a towering figure in cosmology at this time, known for his theory of stellar nucleosynthesis (how chemical elements are created within the nuclear reactions within stars, especially those heavier than helium) and as a staunch defender of the steady-state theory, rejecting the idea that the universe originated in the infinite outrush of the Big Bang. He was also a busy man, and didn't have the capacity to take on Hawking as his research student. Instead, Hawking was assigned to Dennis Sciama (1926–99).

This pairing would actually work greatly to Hawking's advantage. Sciama's reputation soared over time and today he is regarded as one of the fathers of modern cosmology. His own work concentrated on origin theories (he shifted over time from being a steady-state advocate to a believer in the Big Bang) and later on the nature of dark matter. He also proved to be an excellent academic supervisor, to Hawking and others. He would devote time and attention to his students, even if their ideas clashed with his own. Hawking also noted in retrospect that if Hoyle had been his supervisor, he might have been compelled to defend the crumbling walls of the steady-state theory.

CAMBRIDGE

THE DIAGNOSIS

It was at Cambridge that Hawking unleashed the full expression of his mental powers, which were supercharged by the discovery of an ability to work hard, something he had largely avoided at Oxford. But body and mind were evidently going in different directions. The unsettling bodily issues that had arisen at Oxford were getting worse and their impact could no longer be shrugged off or ignored. The problems with co-ordination were spreading into very basic physical actions – tying his own shoelaces soon became an act of will and complexity – and his speech was also becoming slurred.

Nor could he hide the problems from others. When Hawking returned home for his first Christmas holiday, his parents were especially concerned by the changes. A watershed was reached when the family went ice skating, against Hawking's own better judgement. He fell over on the ice and struggled to get himself up off its hard surface. This event, and other observations, led his parents to take him to their doctor, who in turn sent Hawking to St Bartholomew's Hospital in London in the early New Year, to see a specialist consultant and get diagnostic tests.

A battery of painful probings followed. It became clear to the doctors that the young man had a degenerative condition, but apart from ruling out multiple sclerosis (MS) they were at first confounded, and were able to suggest little more than rest and an upped intake of vitamins. But finally, a diagnosis was reached. Hawking had amyotrophic lateral sclerosis (ALS), a type of motor neurone disease. (In the USA this is also known as 'Lou Gehrig disease', after the baseball player of that name who died from the condition.) ALS causes the progressive degeneration of nerve cells in the spinal cord and brain, attacking the muscular control. The early signs are exactly those experienced by Hawking, and over time functionality is degraded severely, terminating in severe issues such as paralysis and problems with breathing and swallowing. Death will often come within three to five years. The doctors who treated Hawking told him that he might have just two years left to live.

It was a terrifying diagnosis. It also seemed horribly unjust, coming at the moment when Hawking was about to plunge into life with maximum energy and seemingly endless opportunities. Hawking's own recollected description of the impact of his diagnosis was captured with a perfectly English sense of restraint: 'The realization that I had an incurable disease that was likely to kill me in a few years was a bit of a shock.'[29] By all accounts, he descended into a black depression, although he would later resist reports that he had taken to alcohol to blunt the trauma. His one consolation appeared to be playing sublime Wagner operas repeatedly and loudly, although a fondness for Wagner appears to have accompanied Hawking throughout his life, in good times as well as bad.

Yet Hawking didn't stay down for long. Indeed, as a general tendancy throughout his unexpectedly long life, Hawking resisted self-pity ferociously. Once over the initial shock of diagnosis, he decided to attack both life and his illness with an iron will. The author John Boslough, who wrote one of the first batch of Hawking autobiographies in the 1980s, said of Hawking that he was the 'toughest man I have ever met'.[30] There is weight in this judgement. Time and again, Hawking would maintain his punishing intellectual workload through illnesses and injuries that would incapacitate most able-bodied persons. He disliked being in any way defined by his ALS. For many of the early years of his illness, he fought doggedly against offers of care support, even to the detriment of loved ones around him. In time, however, his attitude to his illness would soften and shift. For example, in his late career (as we shall see) he acknowledged that his physical condition helped raise his profile and therefore that of his ideas. He also acknowledged that his disability was in some ways an 'asset', as it meant that he could avoid the duties of an able-bodied academic, such as lecturing, teaching undergraduates or sitting on 'tedious and time-consuming committees'. Instead, 'I have been able to devote myself completely to research.'[31]

Such big-picture thinking was a long way in the future for Hawking at Cambridge in 1962–63, but there were other forces preventing him from succumbing to fatalism. His sociable side meant that he began making good friends, some of whom would become lifelong companions. One important early friend was Robert Donovan, another graduate student studying at Trinity Hall with Hawking, although his specialism was chemistry. The two appear to have bonded over conversation, fun and a shared love of Wagner. In Hawking, Donovan saw a sparkling mind backed by a sharp sense of humour and a mischievous streak. Regarding the latter, for example, on Donovan's wedding day Hawking and a friend actually chased the wedding car. The newly-weds shook them off, but found their home festooned in all manner of festive decoration – Hawking had been busy.[32] Donovan became just one of a solid and trusted academic gang around Hawking at Cambridge. Others included George Ellis, who would become the co-author of Hawking's first book, and Martin Rees, who in 1995 became Britain's Astronomer Royal.

MEETING JANE

Alongside friendships, Hawking also found love early on in his Cambridge career. We have already met, briefly, Jane Wilde, who glimpsed the boy Hawking when she was a pupil at St Albans School. By January 1963, Jane was preparing to begin her undergraduate study of languages at Westfield College, part of the University of London. She was still aware of the eccentric Hawking family and their curious elder son. In the late summer of 1962, Jane and her friend had been walking through St Albans one day and had spotted 'a young man with an awkward gait, his head down, his face shielded from the world under an unruly mass of straight brown hair'.[33] She quickly identified him as Stephen Hawking. Her friend mentioned to her that he was known to attend 'ban the bomb' marches – evidently that was something that marked him out as a radical. (Throughout his life, Hawking would argue passionately against the development and stockpiling of nuclear weapons.)

Hawking and Jane Wilde together in a Cambridge punt, 1960s.

It would appear that destiny was determined to force the two together. They next met at a New Year's Eve party in 1963, the event arranged by Jane's old school friend Diana King and her brother. At the party, the 'inwardly shy and very unsure' Jane spotted a familiar figure:

> There, slight of frame, leaning against the wall in a corner with his back to the light, gesticulating with long thin fingers as he spoke – his hair falling across his face over his glasses – and wearing a dusty black-velvet jacket and red-velvet bow tie, stood Stephen Hawking, the young man I had seen lolloping along the street in the summer.[34]

She listened to Hawking regaling those around him with wit and wisdom, possibly a hint of arrogance, the topics ranging from his struggles with supervisors to his research on cosmology. She admits to feeling drawn towards this 'unusual' character. In Jane's later autobiography (from which I am quoting here), she was particularly attracted to his 'sense of humour and his independent personality'.[35] She also warmed to his peculiar physical mannerisms, not least the way he seemed almost to suffocate himself laughing at his own jokes.

Towards the end of the party, Jane and Hawking had the opportunity for a proper introduction and conversation, which seems to have gone well enough that they exchanged contact details. Hawking followed up by inviting Jane to his 21st birthday party at his parental home, which gave Jane the opportunity to view the mysterious Hawking clan behind closed doors. During the evening, however, she did notice Hawking's evident struggles with his own body. A month or so after the event, a friend of hers gave her a version of Hawking's diagnosed condition and its dark prognosis.

The next encounter for Jane and Hawking came when they met on a platform at St Albans train station and shared a 9.00 am train to London. During the journey, she tactfully explained that she had heard of his recent stay in hospital, and she hoped he was recovering. He apparently just 'wrinkled his nose and said nothing'.[36] She quickly understood it was a topic he did not like to discuss. Nevertheless, he asked her out on a more formal date in London. This consisted of dinner and a show at the hallowed Old Vic theatre, clearly an experience designed to impress. That aspiration was jeopardized when, at the end of the evening, Hawking discovered he had no money for their bus fares back to St Albans. Jane would have to take the hit, but when on the bus she discovered she had lost her purse. They were forced to leap off the bus at a set of traffic lights. They quickly deduced that the purse was likely under Jane's seat in the Old Vic, so Hawking led her back there. The main doors were locked, but Hawking found a stage door and they crept into the dimly lit auditorium. They found the purse, at which point all the lights went off and Hawking had to lead Jane, hand-in-hand, through pitch blackness to the exit, after which they fell about laughing.

Evidently, the bus fare incident hadn't knocked the emerging relationship off course. Hawking next took Jane to the exquisitely romantic annual Trinity Hall May Ball, held in June 1963. It was a magical candle-lit evening, but after that their paths separated physically for some time when Jane began her language studies, mainly in London but including periods abroad. They reconnected the following November.

Attraction soon changed into love, although the courtship was erratic at times. In many ways, they were two very different souls. Jane was a committed Christian, whereas Hawking was more of atheist/agnostic leanings, or at least had a radically different concept of the divine, as we will later explore. Jane was sensitive and caring, while Hawking could be headstrong and forceful. Jane was also now more fully aware that Hawking's future, and therefore the future of his romantic partner, would be bound up with the uncertainties of his degenerative illness. She was also aware of Hawking's stubborn attitude towards that illness, an obstinacy that would cause more serious problems years down the road. But despite the differences and the challenges, they had found each other and fallen in love. Hawking proposed marriage, and Jane accepted. He later said of their engagement: 'It gave me something to live for. It made me determined to live.'[37]

MAKING HIS MARK

Academically, the first year at Cambridge was a challenge for Stephen Hawking. He was perfectly up to the task of the graduate work, although he needed to upgrade his mathematical skills quickly (which he did), but the medical interruptions were significant. Frank Hawking, clearly concerned that time was not on his son's side, appealed to Sciama to allow his son to complete the PhD in three years instead of the customary four. Sciama refused, aware that rules were there for a purpose, while also keen to see Hawking's evident brilliance flourish to its fullest extent. Thankfully, Hawking's condition stabilized enough for him to immerse himself fully in his studies.

CAMBRIDGE

Postgraduate studies at Cambridge at this time encouraged exploratory, independent thought under a loose timetable (dependent on the supervisor, of course). The students at the individual Cambridge colleges were not siloed; they mixed intellectually with other colleges, fostering ideas, seeking solutions and inspiration, attending lectures. The supervisors would benchmark progress with student seminars and assessment of written work. A key goal for Hawking and his peers was to define a suitably impressive and important topic for the PhD thesis, which was meant to display the student's original and rigorous research.

At first, Hawking studied mainly at the Phoenix Wing of the great Cavendish Laboratory, one of the most important institutional centres for theoretical and experimental research in the history of modern physics. In 1964, however, he moved his office to the newer and glossier Department of Applied Mathematics and Theoretical Physics (DAMTP) on Silver Street, founded only a few years earlier in 1959.

As Hawking bedded into his research, he began to demonstrate the logical brilliance and intellectual boldness for which he would become known. There is one particularly famous incident during these early years of postgraduate research that marked him out as one to watch. At the DAMTP building, he worked next to another exceptional graduate student, Jayant Narlikar; Hawking had previously taken a summer school course under Narlikar. Through their interactions, Hawking had learned that Narlikar's supervisor, Fred Hoyle, was working up to presenting a paper in which he would defend his steady-state theory against the observational data that was supposedly challenging it. Hawking found the opportunity to look in detail at the mathematics behind Hoyle's arguments.

He pinpointed gaps and problems, and spent time reworking the mathematics more to his satisfaction. Prior to the publication of the paper, Hoyle gave a presentation of his theories to the Royal Society in June 1964, an event that Hawking attended. The presentation completed, the venerable Hoyle asked if there were any questions from the mostly respectful floor. Hawking, a postgraduate student in his early 20s, stood up and publicly stated that Hoyle's theories were erroneous. Hoyle, starting to bristle, asked how he knew that. 'Because I calculated it', replied Hawking.

Hawking was not just posturing. He had by this time been working with the likes of George Ellis (a research fellow and lecturer in DAMTP), using the revelations of the CMBR to rethink the origins of the universe. Hawking considered the theories that said the universe's current inflationary phase was actually a rebound from a previous contraction phase. According to this model, the beginning of the inflation, or the end of contraction, was not an infinite singularity, but rather a high-density finite state. Hawking felt that it was in this 'fundamental question' that he would find 'just what I needed to complete my PhD thesis'.[38] At first Hawking focused on a current hot topic: whether forces of rotation could cause the universe to bounce out from a contraction phase. He ultimately decided that the answer to that question was 'no', but other theoretically deep intellectual challenges soon presented themselves.

Hawking's ongoing research focus was shaped by his response to the work of another brilliant mind, that of the mathematician and mathematical physicist Roger Penrose, a reader (a title for an eminent research scholar) at Birkbeck College, University of London. Sciama's research team (which included Hawking) had begun exchanges with Penrose over his theories, with the Cambridge-based group travelling down to London for in-depth discussions. This brought some moments of practical chaos. In one incident, Brandon Carter, one of the Cambridge team, remembered he and his colleagues having to jump off a moving train pulling away from the platform so that they could manhandle Hawking – who had been struggling to get to the train door – physically aboard.

The Cambridge scholars discovered that Penrose was making big waves in cosmology, particularly in papers that applied general relativity to spacetime singularities.[39] As Hawking explored the implications of Penrose's calculations, he realized Penrose had demonstrated that once a collapsing star reaches a critical stage, it inevitably leads to the formation of a singularity. This singularity represents a point where the curvature of spacetime becomes infinite, effectively marking the limits of our current understanding of time and space. Hawking felt that this in itself was not entirely new thinking, but was already largely encapsulated in existing theory (think Oppenheimer–Snyder). But Penrose had more to reveal, plus Hawking was inspired to question whether Penrose's models of singularities could be plausibly extended from beyond stars and black holes to the wider universe. Could the universe itself have begun in a singularity, deduced by winding back the inflationary state of all matter to its origin point?

Here there was a problem that Penrose and Hawking had to address. In 1963, two Soviet scientists, Evgeny Lifshitz and Isaak Khalatnikov, argued that they had found a solution to Einstein's field equations, suggesting that the formation of singularities was highly unlikely under realistic conditions. They proposed that singularities could theoretically form, but only under ideal conditions, such as a perfectly symmetrical star. In reality, imperfections like variations in pressure or velocity would prevent singularities from forming. Applying this idea to the wider universe, they suggested that irregularities in space (known as 'perturbations') would prevent a cosmic singularity, implying that the universe might not have a singular beginning or end, but rather an infinite past and future. The Friedmann–Robertson–Walker (FRW) model, another influential theory, predicted a universal singularity under Einstein's general relativity, but only assuming a universe that was perfectly homogeneous and isotropic (the same in all directions).

Penrose was the first to rise to the challenge of these theories by showing mathematically that a singularity could form in the collapse of *any* massive body, even if it had imperfections or lacked perfect symmetry. This work demonstrated that singularities were a feature inherent in general relativity, not just an outcome of idealized models. Hawking picked up Penrose's ideas and ran with them. He began applying the stellar theories to cosmology, investigating the possibility that a *universal* singularity, such as that which could have occurred prior to the Big Bang, might also be a core feature of general relativity, independent of the assumptions of homogeneity and isotropy. In 1965, Hawking published a short paper with George Ellis entitled 'Singularities in homogeneous world models'.[40] They argued that singularities were indeed a possibility in a spatially homogeneous anisotropic model; *anisotropic* means that something has a range of physical values when measured in different directions.

Building upon this position, Hawking's next step was to attempt to deepen the understanding of singularities themselves. Again, collaboration with Penrose provided a stepping stone. In 1965, Penrose advanced his theory of the 'trapped surface', showing that a singularity could form without the need for perfect symmetry in the collapsing object. He demonstrated mathematically that the intense curvature of spacetime caused by mass and energy leads to the inward convergence of light rays within a trapped surface. This means that, much like railway lines converging through perspective, the paths of light waves in spacetime are progressively bent inwards towards each other. Light under these conditions forms itself into a pear-shaped 'light cone', the centre of the pear's base representing the point at which light finally meets at a point: the singularity. Another, less elegant, analogy used to describe the model is that of people (representing light waves) tumbling down the sides of a steep valley (representing spacetime), all eventually meeting at the same point on the valley floor.

Penrose rigorously argued that the trapped surface model showed that a singularity could occur in general conditions, not just in perfect states. Hawking, in his October 1965 paper 'Occurrence of Singularities in Open Universes', showed how Penrose's theory could be applied to prove generic singularities in inflationary cosmological models.[41] To give a little more context, in his autobiography Hawking notes that the theories he and Penrose developed worked on the assumption that the universe has what is known as a 'Cauchy surface'. Named after the French mathematician Augustin-Louis Cauchy (1789–1857), a Cauchy surface is a concept in general relativity explained by Hawking as 'a surface that intersects every particle path once and once only'.[42] The particle path relationship means that a Cauchy surface is a type of surface in spacetime that contains all the information necessary to predict the past and future of the universe, based on the laws of physics. The Cauchy surface thus allows for a deterministic evolution of spacetime.

The Cauchy surface represented a problem for Hawking, because a singularity would actually represent the failure of the Cauchy surface model; a singularity was by its very nature the point at which deterministic predictions broke down, and which in turn challenged the predictability inherent in general relativity itself. Hawking's work highlighted these limits, demonstrating that while Cauchy surfaces allow for deterministic predictions in much of spacetime, singularities mark the boundaries where such predictions can no longer be made. Thus Hawking introduced the ideas of the 'Cauchy horizon', a point at which the laws of physics no longer apply.

Hawking's work was ambitious, with the potential to reframe theoretical physics in cosmology. In his autobiography, Hawking explained how over the subsequent five years he worked with Penrose and theoretical physicist Robert Geroch to 'develop the theory of causal structure in general relativity'. It was by his own admission a heady time, defined by the liberty of exploring an intellectual space in which there were few others: 'It was a wonderful feeling, having a whole field virtually to ourselves.'[43] His work in the mid-1960s culminated in a finalized PhD thesis. While many doctoral theses go on to languish largely unread on library shelves (the author includes his own here), Hawking's is still essential reading for those wanting to understand his ideas and the state of cosmological research at this point in time. The abstract to the thesis reveals the ambitious scope of the work across its 119 pages:

> Some implications and consequences of the expansion of the universe are examined. In Chapter 1 it is shown that this expansion creates grave difficulties for the Hoyle–Narlikar theory of gravita-

tion. Chapter 2 deals with perturbations of an expanding homogeneous and isotropic universe. The conclusion is reached that galaxies cannot be formed as a result of the growth of perturbations that were initially small. The propagation and absorption of gravitational radiation is also investigated in this approximation. In Chapter 3 gravitational radiation in an expanding universe is examined by a method of asymptotic expansions. The 'peeling off' behaviour and the asymptotic group are derived. Chapter 4 deals with the occurrence of singularities in cosmological models. It is shown that a singularity is inevitable provided that certain very general conditions are satisfied.[44]

The quality and importance of his thesis meant that the award of a doctorate was never in doubt, and thus in 1966 Stephen Hawking became Dr Stephen Hawking. But Hawking's thesis, and the several papers he wrote in the mid-1960s, were just the first stirrings of a tremendous intellectual energy. In his 2001 book *The Universe in a Nutshell*, which acted as a follow-up to his enormously impactful *A Brief History of Time*, Hawking explained that he and Penrose had reached the point at which they 'could prove that in the mathematical model of general relativity, time must have a beginning in what is called the Big Bang'.[45] In 1966, he published the essay 'Singularities and the geometry of spacetime', in which he aimed 'to investigate certain aspects of the geometry of the spacetime manifold in the General Theory of Relativity with particular reference to the occurrence of singularities in cosmological solutions and their relation with other global properties'.[46] In this paper, he argued that his results 'seem to imply either that the General Theory of Relativity breaks down or that there could be particles whose histories did not exist before (or after) a certain time. The author's own opinion is that the theory probably does break down, but only when quantum gravitational effects become important.'[47]

Here was an important evolution in Hawking's future direction, the fusion of general relativity with quantum mechanics, an approach that would later lead to some of his most high-profile academic achievements. The paper was entered into the 1966 Adams Prize competition, a prestigious annual prize awarded by the Faculty of Mathematics at St John's College in the University of Cambridge, first awarded in the mid-19th century. (It is named after the British mathematician and astronomer John Couch Adams, 1819–92.) Although the prize that year deservedly went to Roger Penrose, for his paper 'An analysis of the structure of space-time', both Hawking and Narlikar were given additional prizes for outstanding work. Two years later, however, Hawking and Penrose jointly penned a paper, 'On Gravitational Collapse and Cosmology', and submitted it to another competition, this time run by the Gravity Research Foundation. The abstract of the paper illustrated how they were both tightening up and advancing their understanding of singularities:

> We present a new theorem on space-time singularities. On the basis of the Einstein (or Brans-Dicke) theory, and without using any Cauchy surface assumption, we show (essentially from the property that gravitation is always attractive) that singularities will occur if there exists <u>either</u> a compact spacelike hypersurface <u>or</u> a closed trapped surface <u>or</u> a point whose past light-cone starts converging again. The first condition would be satisfied by any spatially closed universe, the second by a collapsing star and the

third by the observable portion of our actual universe – as we shall show follows from observations of the microwave background radiation.[48]

The paper was a very strong submission, but it failed to win the top award, although Hawking and Penrose did take home the second prize. Seen from the perspective of his later success, Hawking later expressed the somewhat prickly view that the other essays in the competition did not show much 'enduring value', unlike his own.

The last statement in the abstract, connecting the mathematical theory of spacetime singularities with the observable and measurable evidence of the CMBR, was another important part of Hawking's work from the late 1960s. Indeed, the same year (1968) that he and Penrose submitted their paper to the Gravity Research Foundation, he and George Ellis wrote a paper entitled 'The Cosmic Black-Body Radiation and the Existence of Singularities in our Universe', published in the *Astrophysical Journal*.[49] In this they demonstrated how the CMBR detected just a few years previously provided observational evidence to support their arguments about singularities. But the pattern of radiation in the universe also threw them a problem, one that Hawking wrestled with from the 1960s into the new millennium. It would be called the 'horizon problem'.

The CMBR implied that the universe had begun in a very hot, very dense state, before inflating outwards to form the universe we see today. That universe, however, is full of localized irregularities, such as galaxies, stars and planets, whereas the temperature of the CMBR was uniform in whatever direction the measurements were taken in. This was suspicious. In *A Brief History of Time*, Hawking described this as akin to giving a large number of students an exam paper and them all coming up with the same answer, which suggests that they were speaking with one another all along. The cosmological equivalent of this problem is that there would not have been enough time since the Big Bang for light to travel from one distant region of space to the other. This meant, under the principles of special relativity, that if nothing is faster than the speed of light, then there was no way that other information (such as thermal temperature) could be transferred uniformly across the different regions of the universe, 'unless for some unexplained reason they happened to start out with the same temperature'.[50]

Alongside this conundrum, Hawking listed some important others. Why was the early universe so hot? Why is the universe, billions of years after its birth, still expanding at nearly that critical rate it began with? What were the origins of the density fluctuations in spacetime that causes the emergence of 'local irregularities', such as stars and galaxies? Hawking would tackle such issues from various different angles over the subsequent decades. To give these some additional context, however, it is worth exploring how Hawking saw the various options for the universe's development from the Big Bang, as outlined in *A Brief History of Time*. These will form important frameworks for our evolving discussion.

We have already seen, on page 55, how Alexander Friedmann revealed that the inflationary universe looks the same in every direction (remember the expanding currant cake), with the galaxies all moving directly away from each other. Taking Friedmann's assumptions, and utilizing the work of other scientists such as Howard P. Robertson (1903–61) and Arthur Walker (1909–2001), three models were developed to explain the direction of universal expansion. Friedmann's own model had the galaxies of the universe expanding outwards from the Big Bang, but with the gravitational attraction steadily slowing them until the expansion ceased and the inflation went into reverse. The terminus to this process is the Big Crunch, when all matter comes back together again at a single point. Hawking describes this as the movement from point zero to maximum expansion and back again to point zero, and is graphed as an inverse U shape, the x axis representing time and the y axis representing the distance of separation of the galaxies. This model represents what we call a 'closed universe'. The second model is, by contrast, that of the 'open universe'. In this model, the universe is in a state of such rapid acceleration that gravitational attraction is not sufficient to prevent inflation. Although Hawking notes that gravity can slow the acceleration, the universe nevertheless keeps on expanding for infinite time. Finally, the third option is the 'flat' model. In this model, the galactic movement and gravitational attraction exactly balance one another, thus the universe avoids a Big Crunch while the motion of the galaxies gets smaller and smaller, although never entirely ceasing.

The three models, as we will come to discover, have some important conceptual relationships to spacetime, as Hawking clarifies:

> In the first kind of Friedmann model, which expands and recollapses, space is bent in on itself, like the surface of the Earth. It is therefore finite in extent. In the second kind of model, which expands forever, space is bent the other way, like the surface of a saddle. So in this case space is infinite. Finally in the third kind of Friedmann model, with just the critical rate of expansion, space is flat (and therefore is also infinite).[51]

For the general reader, there are evidently some leaps of intuition, imagination and knowledge contained in this paragraph, some of which we will address in the later development of Hawking's theories. For now, however, bear in mind that the nature of the inflationary model of the universe has a fundamental connection to the nature of spacetime.

STRUGGLE AND SUCCESS

While his mind was making leaps in scientific thought, Hawking also had regular life to handle. Easier said than done. Hawking was now engaged to be married, but what he also needed was a secure short-to medium-term financial future. With marriage, and possibly children, on the horizon Hawking simply needed a job. It was also imperative that he find new accommodation, a home that also needed to accommodate his long-term physical atrophy.

To solve the job part of the equation, in 1964, while still pursuing his PhD, Hawking applied for a paid research fellowship at Gonville and Caius College in Cambridge University. His superlative academic performance helped him secure the position. With financial stability now in place, Jane and Stephen were finally married. The wedding took place on 14 July 1965. It was a simple civil ceremony, but the following day they had a religious service in the beautiful chapel of Trinity Hall, with Donovan as best man. The newly-weds then took off for a honeymoon in Suffolk, although this was kept necessarily short, as soon after the pair headed out to Cornell University in New York State, where Stephen attended a conference on general relativity. It would be the first of very many trips to the USA made by Hawking as a married man and as a scientist of growing international repute.

On their return from abroad, the Hawkings had a somewhat stressful time finding new accommodation suited to them as a married couple. They stayed for three days in a hostel for graduate students, but during that time found a small house available to rent on St Mary's Way. This house was only about 100 yards from the DAMTP. This position was ideal, given Stephen's increasing struggle with walking. They would live there for three months in total, before moving to another house on the street.

Hawking took up his fellowship position in October 1965. On some levels, life was working out perfectly for the young scientist. He was happily married, his academic work was highly regarded, he had found employment, his future career path looked strong, and he was living in a comfortable house in one of England's most beautiful cities. But there remained the matter of his health. Here, things were not good, and it was clear that they would only get worse. His co-ordination was punctuated by spasms and clumsiness. The act of writing became a torturous struggle as his fingers began to curl up and stiffen. Even writing out his own fellowship application was a feat of co-operation. He intended for Jane to write up his words, but she broke her wrist while twisting to music at a 'midweek hop', so it took a whole weekend to produce the application using her functioning hand.[52] Walking was increasingly problematic. Now he moved slowly and precariously, assisted by a cane; on the day of his wedding, he replaced the cane with a more dashing umbrella. The illness was also starting to assault critical body functions. His speech was becoming strained and slow, eating away at his ability to communicate with others. More alarming, the disease began attacking the fine separation humans have between breathing and eating. While at Cornell, Hawking experienced a sudden and threatening choking fit, only rectified by a sharp blow on the back from Jane. These choking episodes would increase in frequency.

The university was very aware of Hawking's mounting physical challenges. Professor Sciama even managed to arrange twice-weekly physical therapy sessions for Hawking, paid for by the Institute of Physics. But by the late 1960s, by which time a cane had been replaced by two crutches, it was clear that Hawking was fighting a losing battle against the loss of mobility. It was, however, a battle that he kept fighting with determination. His biographer Kitty Ferguson wrote that one visitor to the Hawking household saw Stephen take a full 15 minutes to ascend the stairs to the upper floor, doggedly refusing any offers of assistance. His problems with speech had now become so severe that he could no longer give lectures or hold seminars. Given the very nature of academic duties, this issue could have been career threatening, but again Hawking's intellectual brilliance secured his future. Hawking's fellowship was due to end in 1969, but the academic staff at Gonville and Caius College recognized that they did not want Hawking's rising star to shine over another university. Thus Hawking was given a specially created 'Fellowship for Distinction in Science', and he went on the staff roster for the university's Institute of Theoretical Astronomy, which had been created by Fred Hoyle in 1967.

Life-changing events came thick and fast for Hawking in the second half of the 1960s. Not least, he became a father. The couple's first child, Robert, was born on 28 May 1967. Robert would be the first of three children born to Jane and Stephen: a daughter, Lucy Hawking, arrived on 2 November 1970 and Timothy Hawking entered as the youngest of the pack on 15 April 1979. Fatherhood was fully and emotionally embraced by Hawking. This book will not expand in much detail on the relationship between father and offspring, as the Hawking children have done so themselves in many writings and interviews (see the Bibliography for some recommended titles). But by all accounts, he appears attentive and loving towards his children when he was in their presence. Overall, Hawking had a genuine respect for children's inquisitive natures, and always seemed prepared to spend time answering tough cosmological questions from his own children or from their friends. Hawking had a belief, expressed in his published work, that a lack of scientific education should not prevent people from being offered unpatronizing and accurate answers to the big scientific questions. Furthermore, he was adept at finding the phrasing and analogies that helped overcome knowledge barriers. Late in life, Hawking would write a series of children's science books with his daughter Lucy (the *George's Secret Key to the Universe* series), and was apparently every bit as serious about the scientific accuracy in those volumes as in his own academic works. He also took education seriously; children, he understood, were the future of science.

Family responsibilities were going through a distinct inflationary phase. At the same time, Hawking was putting in long hours at work, fuelled by a singular passion for the subject. Combined with the problems induced by ALS, his scientific drive meant that Jane's personal and professional life became squeezed ever tighter. Jane had to take the pressure of raising children physically almost single-handed, as her husband had severe limitations on what practicalities he could shoulder around the house. Furthermore, although Jane was a capable intellect in her own right, it soon became clear that Stephen's exceptional mind was going to take precedence. For example, Robert was just an infant when the family made a seven-week trip to the USA for Hawking to attend a summer school in Seattle. Hawking's rising reputation was signified by frequent international travel, particularly to the USA but eventually to all manner of destinations, often including long-haul flights. For Jane, the logistics of managing Hawking, the children and her own ongoing pursuits – she was by this time doing a PhD in medieval Spanish literature – became fraught, and would in time call for more drastic practical solutions. The problems inherent in balancing her life with that of her husband would only increase over the years, with significant consequences.

CHAPTER 4

INTO THE BLACK HOLE

Having already challenged scientific conceptions of the origins of the universe, Hawking next turned his attention more directly to another long-standing interest: black holes. In many ways, Hawking's work on black holes would become the theoretical signature of his career.

EUREKA MOMENT

Back in 1965, Roger Penrose's exploration of black holes had formulated the concept of the trapped surface, one in which light around the black hole was unable to escape the gravitational warping of spacetime. Penrose also worked on developing the concept of the 'apparent horizon', a boundary within a black hole where light rays are momentarily parallel before being pulled inwards. Penrose and Hawking subsequently collaborated to explore black hole topography further, leading to a deeper understanding of the 'event horizon'.

The event horizon term, now popularized in sci-fi culture, was a bold new insight in the 1960s. It represents the outer boundary of a black hole, beyond which nothing can escape, and plays a central role in defining the black hole's structure. It is the point at which light hovers on the edge of the radius of the black hole, unable to escape the gravitational pull. As Hawking describes it, it coincides with the 'paths of light rays that just fail to escape from the black hole'.[53] Because light photons are unable to escape at this point, the event horizon is forever hidden from the observer, as there are no photons to reach his or her eyes. (In contrast to the event horizon, which is a boundary around the black hole, the apparent horizon can shift its position depending on the influence of matter and energy around the black hole.)

Given that so much of black holes is invisible to observational technology, there remained the question: How can we know that black holes exist? John Wheeler had demonstrated that there were actually three observable, or at least detectable, features of a black hole: its total mass; its electrical charge (if it has one); and its speed of rotation or angular momentum. Thus, the presence of a black hole can be inferred from gravitational effects on surrounding matter, such as the movement of nearby stars and the radiation emitted by material falling into them. But there were no external signs of its presence, a fact that Wheeler pithily captured in the phrase: 'Black holes have no hair!'

As Hawking described it, his explorations of black holes began in 1970 in what he called a 'eureka moment' just a few days after the birth of his daughter Lucy. 'While getting into bed, I realized that I could apply to black holes the causal structure theory I had developed for singularity theorems.'[54] He was quickly up and running in the new direction. In 1971, Hawking and British theoretical physicist Gary Gibbons published a paper entitled 'Evidence for black holes in binary star systems' in the internationally respected journal *Nature*. In the paper, Hawking provided an evidentiary basis for black holes, specifically that in binary star systems (a system in which two stars are gravitationally bound to each other in orbit) if one star collapsed to form a black hole it would strip mass from its partner. This proposal eventually led, in 1974, to a famous bet between Hawking and his close friend Kip Thorne, Professor of Theoretical Physics at the California Institute of Technology (Caltech). The bet revolved around whether a specific binary star system about 6,000 light-years from Earth, designated Cygnus X-1, was a black hole. If it was, Hawking would be obliged to give Thorne a one-year subscription to the men's magazine *Penthouse*. If it was not, then Thorne had to pay for a four-year subscription to the investigative British newspaper *Private Eye*. For reference, in 1990 Hawking conceded the bet. Hawking, as we will see, had a predilection for making wagers.

In his writings about black holes, Hawking has perfectly captured the general weirdness of time and space around the event horizon. In *A Brief History*, for example, he explains that if you were watching a black hole collapse then, according to relativity, there is no absolute time involved. To demonstrate, he asks us to imagine an astronaut standing on the surface of a collapsing star, sending a signal every second to his spaceship, which is orbiting the star at a safe distance. At 11.00 am, the star collapses below the critical limit, and thus, given that light itself now cannot escape the pull, all signals from the astronaut will now fail to reach the spaceship. The real oddity about the event from the point of view of the spaceship crew is that up to 10.59.59 am, the signals from the astronaut would be getting longer, but only fractionally so. But between 10.59.59 and 11.00 am, the crew would have to wait forever for the signal emitted at 11.00 am, as the light waves of the signal would now be spread out over an infinite period of time. The light from the star, meanwhile, would get 'redder and redder and fainter and fainter' until the only thing left would be the black hole, albeit still exerting the same gravitational attraction on the spaceship as previously. And what of the astronaut himself? Hawking was often asked the question, 'What would happen if someone fell into a black hole?' The answer was generally that the gravitational difference between the astronaut's head and his feet as he slipped over the event horizon would turn him into spaghetti.

Hawking's work on black holes was unrelenting, and over the 1970s and 1980s he expanded our thinking about these phenomena, often through working collaboratively with the likes of Thorne, Penrose, Wheeler and others. In his individual paper 'Gravitational Radiation from Colliding Black Holes', published in May 1971, he demonstrated that if two black holes collide and merge then the resulting area of the event horizon was as great or greater than the masses of the individual black holes.[55] This model became known as the 'Second Law of Black Holes'. (Note that in 2016 observational data from the convergence of two black holes was proved consistent with Hawking's theory.) He also worked on the mathematical shape of black holes.

The actual shape of a black hole opened up yet another significant area of exploration for Hawking, in what was called the 'cosmic censorship hypothesis'. This theory was first proposed by Roger Penrose, and it specifically addressed the fact that all the known laws of physics broke down in a black hole's singularity. This was a mind-bending prospect in itself, but Penrose argued that it also threatened the very predictability of the universe – the presence of black holes jeopardized the orderliness of space and time. To prevent this happening, however, Penrose theorized that the singularity of a black hole was 'censored' behind the event horizon. The event horizon prevented a 'naked' singularity, i.e. one that could be observed directly from the outside.

Penrose put forward two versions of the cosmic censorship hypothesis. The 'weak' version basically offered the reassurance that the singularity was simply hidden from the observer by the event horizon. In that sense, the laws of physics could be breaking down within the black hole, but that didn't matter to outside observers since they couldn't see it anyway, and their universe continued obeying the regular laws. The 'strong' version, however, was that the singularities are not only hidden from view, but there is no way in which they can influence external spacetime, regardless of how the observer perceives the phenomenon.

Enter Hawking. Inspired by Penrose's theory, Hawking made a wager with Kip Thorne and John Preskill, both of Caltech, that the cosmic censorship hypothesis was correct: Hawking was for; Thorne and Preskill were against. The stakes were undeniably odd. The loser had to give the winner 'clothing to cover the winner's nakedness', but embroidered with a concessionary message of the winner's choice.[56] It was another of Hawking's long-term bets. In fact, this one was not resolved until 1997, when advanced computer simulations did indeed show the possibility of a black hole singularity *without* an event horizon, although the chances of that happening were formidably unlikely. So, Hawking was the loser. His forfeit was to provide a T-shirt featuring a naked and shapely cartoon woman, her modesty covered strategically with a towel, also bearing the inscription 'Nature Abhors a Naked Singularity'. Science and humour were never too far apart in Hawking's world-view. He also had an eye for a classically voluptuous figure; his office wall was typically decorated with a life-size picture of Marilyn Monroe.

Hawking's next contribution to black-hole theory came in 1971, with his paper entitled 'Gravitationally Collapsed Objects of Very

Low Mass' in the *Monthly Notices of the Royal Astronomical Society*. In it, he presented in the abstract, 'It is suggested that there may be a large number of gravitationally collapsed objects of mass 10−5 g upwards which were formed as a result of fluctuations in the early Universe.'[57] We are typically used to thinking of black holes as enormous cosmological features. Some of the 'super-massive' black holes, for example, can be hundreds of thousands, millions, or even billions of times greater in mass than our own Sun. In his new work, Hawking modelled black holes at the opposite extreme – the smallest could be the size of the nucleus of an atom. He called these tiny phenomena 'primordial black holes'.

There was an obvious problem here. The size of the primordial black holes meant that they were wildly below the Chandrasekhar limit. But Hawking demonstrated mathematically how they could form under conditions of super-high temperature and extraordinary compression ... such as occurred in the Big Bang and the beginning of the universe. Although primordial black holes could have been created in that event, they might still be present today, albeit even smaller than they were at their birth (for reasons we shall soon explore). Their theoretical presence was important, however, because they also demonstrated that the early universe had to have irregularities in its density; specific regions necessarily had to be denser than the average for primordial black holes to form. Hawking had given us another great mathematical glimpse into the unknown.

HAWKING RADIATION

By 1973, Hawking had already changed the scientific understanding of both cosmological origins and black holes, those two lines of research feeding productively into one another. But in 1973, Hawking offered the world an ambitious theory that transformed the foundations of physics. It also put Hawking on the first rungs of the ladder to public stardom, an exceptionally rare thing indeed in theoretical physics. Although his theory was in its detail well beyond the cognition of the vast majority of us, it ironically helped to make him a much-recognized figure in non-scientific popular culture.

Think back to Chapter 2 and our discussion of entropy, the core measure within the second law of thermodynamics. By the early 1970s, it was already understood that the mass of a black hole would increase as matter was drawn into it. But if we take that fact in relation to entropy, we have a problem. Hawking provides an explanation of that problem in *A Brief History of Time*. Remember his box full of disordered gas molecules? Imagine throwing that box into a black hole. That particular unit of entropy has now disappeared from the universe into the singularity, so for the universe does that mean that the inviolable second law has in fact been violated? Do black holes reduce the total entropy of the universe?

In December 1970, Hawking was attending the Texas Symposium of Relativistic Astrophysics, another date in his busy international diary. At the conference, he presented his theory that the event horizon of a black hole could never reduce in size, but only increase in size as matter fell into the void. There was a dissenting voice present, however. Jacob Bekenstein, a research student from Princeton, argued that the event horizon was in fact a measure of the entropy in the black hole. The implication of this, as explained by Hawking, was that 'As matter carrying entropy fell into a black hole, the area of its event horizon would go up, so the sum of the entropy of matter outside black holes and the area of the horizons would never go down.'[58] Hawking would spend the next two years arguing against this position; he described himself as 'irritated' by what he saw as a misapplication of his theory of the static or expanding event horizon. His position culminated in a paper jointly written with Australian theoretical physicist Brandon Carter and American physicist Jim Bardeen. A key problem for Bekenstein, they highlighted, was that if a black hole exhibited entropy, it would also emit heat and radiation in accordance with the second law (heat transfer and radiation are processes that can result in changes in entropy), but the gravitational pull of the black hole was, as we know, so great that nothing can escape its force.

In time, by his own admission, Hawking would be proved wrong. The journey to that discovery began in August–September 1973, when Hawking and Jane made a work/pleasure trip to Eastern Europe, first stopping in Warsaw before journeying on to Moscow. In the Russian capital, he met two esteemed Soviet physicists, Yakov Zeldovich and Alexander Starobinsky. By applying the uncertainty principle from quantum theory, they had demonstrated that rotating black holes specifically could, indeed, create and emit particles. How was this so?

We can start unpacking this using Hawking's analogy of a pendulum. Fusing quantum theory with Maxwell's electromagnetic field, we can picture an electromagnetic wavelength like a pendulum swinging from one value to another. If the pendulum simply hangs straight down, completely static and in its lowest energy state, it actually violates Heisenberg's uncertainty principle: the tip of the pendulum has a definite position (zero) and also a definite velocity (zero). As you may remember, the uncertainty principle means that you can measure the position of a particle or the velocity of a particle, but more precision in one measurement means less precision in the other. Instead, the pendulum's lowest energy state must actually include minimal amounts of fluctuation from the zero point. While swinging pendulums might not appear relevant to our discussion, they do, as we will see, suggest the possibility of black hole radiation.

Hawking immediately saw promise in what Zeldovich and Starobinsky had done, but sensed that there were problems in their mathematics. Back in Cambridge, he set to work and actually came to an even more radical conclusion, namely that even non-rotating black holes could emit radiation. It looked like Bekenstein was right.

So given the very nature of black holes, how could anything escape its voracious intake? We come back to the uncertainty principle and pendulums. Although the vacuum of space appears absolute, it is not. In fact, vacuum fluctuations along the lines of quantum mechanics mean that as the value of a field oscillates between positive and negative energy, pairs of particles (e.g. photons and neutrons) are created. Hawking terms these particles 'virtual particles', not because they don't exist, but rather because they 'cannot be observed directly, but their indirect effects can be measured, and they agree with theoretical predictions to a remarkable degree of accuracy'.[59] These form particle/anti-particle pairs that come into existence together, then separate, then come back together forcibly and annihilate each other, all in minuscule fractions of time. The duration of time they exist in is rigorously set by the Heisenberg Uncertainty Principle: H < Dt x DE such that Dt < H/DE. This means that the more energy the pairs contain (DE), the shorter is their lifetime to avoid detection (Dt).

Hawking took that insight into the dimension of black holes. He modelled the theory that if a pair of particles formed just outside the event horizon of a black hole, the particle carrying negative energy could be drawn into the black hole, while its positive partner escaped outward, becoming a free 'real' particle. The black hole therefore prevents the two particles reuniting and annihilating one another. The crucial implication of all this is that to an observer the black hole is behaving like a hot body, emitting radiation (the escaping positive particles) 'with a temperature proportional to the gravitational field on the horizon – the boundary – of the black hole'.[60]

In the world of physics, under the current state of understanding, this was wild stuff. Stephen Hawking's theory of black hole radiation showed that black holes are not completely black but instead emit radiation due to quantum effects near their event horizons. This radiation carries energy away from the black hole. In this process, the black hole loses energy and, equivalently, mass, as per Einstein's equation $E = mc^2$. Over time, this loss of mass could cause a black hole to shrink and eventually evaporate completely. In the final stages of this evaporation process, the black hole could release a burst of high-energy particles back out into the universe.

It was one thing for Hawking to formulate these radical theories. It was quite another to take them into the public domain. For those outside academia, it might be difficult to understand the thin ice over which Hawking's reputation was skating. His models might completely revolutionize the scientific understanding of black holes. Or they might bring him ridicule and failure. He first tested out his ideas gently on friends and receptive colleagues, then presented them formally at the Second Quantum Gravity Conference at the Rutherford Appleton Laboratory near Oxford. His paper was entitled 'Black Hole Explosions?' – the question mark suggests that he was hedging his bets a little.

Once Hawking finished reading his paper, the audience sat in a state of mixed confusion. Some were even embarrassed for Hawking. Few took it as far as the moderator, the respected Professor John G. Taylor (1913–2012), who stood up and declared to the room: 'Sorry Stephen, this is absolute rubbish!'

Immediate opinions notwithstanding, Hawking's theories about black hole radiation and destruction remained well argued and undeniably exciting. On 1 March 1974, the renowned *Nature* magazine published Hawking's paper. Like cosmological expansion from an intellectual Big Bang, Hawking's ideas became the topic of animated debate and argument throughout the world of theoretical physics and cosmology. There were many initial opponents, but progressively the integrity of Hawking's calculations and deductions was accepted. Radiation and mass/energy loss became part of the standard understanding of black holes, and remains so to this day. The phenomenon Hawking had defined would even take his name – it became known officially as 'Hawking radiation'. Hawking had now gone from being a respected upcoming physicist to one of the world's leading scientific thinkers. It was the beginning of his rise to fame.

Recognition came quickly. Shortly after Hawking read out his paper at Oxford, he was elected in 1974 as a Fellow of the Royal Society (FRS). The Royal Society is a prestigious scientific academy in the UK, founded in the 17th century. Its fellows have included some of the greatest names in scientific thought, including Sir Isaac Newton. At just 32 years old, Hawking was one of the youngest members of the society across its illustrious 300-year history. Within three years, he took a professorship at Cambridge. Also, he was starting to get wider press and media coverage beyond academia. He was interviewed or acknowledged in the columns of broadsheet newspapers, and even featured in TV documentaries. One BBC documentary, *The Key to the Universe*, broadcast in 1977, did fly-on-the-wall filming inside DAMTP. At one point, it showed a typically austere Cambridge classroom of the 1970s. The camera pans across the room of earnest physicists. In the centre, at the back, sits Hawking, bound to his wheelchair but at this stage still possessing the power of speech and some movement. The narrator (Nigel Calder) introduces him:

> Black holes have gripped the imagination of a young generation of theorists like these at Cambridge University. As ideas are stretched to the limit the acknowledged leader in black hole theory is Stephen Hawking. He and another British theorist, Roger Penrose, laid down the basic principles ten years ago [when] they said the black hole would possess at its centre an even stranger object, all the matter of a star collapsed to a geometric point, a singularity where gravity crushes particles out of existence. The grave physical handicap makes Stephen Hawking's work all the more remarkable; for thirteen years, since his student days, he's fought a wasting disease of nerve and muscle.[61]

The camera then cuts to Hawking's home, where we watch he and Jane play with their children in the garden; Hawking chases a cycling Robert around the lawn from his wheelchair. The narrator points out the lack of self-pity on Hawking's part: '"With a physical handicap," he says, "you can't afford a psychological one."' Towards the end of the broadcast, Hawking himself speaks to camera, although his voice is overlaid with that of a BBC speaker for clarity. He was already showing his talent for creating media-friendly lines that played well with the imagination of the general public: 'The Big Bang is like a black hole explosion but on a much larger scale. By finding out how a black hole creates matter we may discover how the Big Bang created all the matter in the universe. The singularity of the Big Bang seems to be a frontier beyond which we cannot go, yet we can't help asking what lies beyond the Big Bang. Why does the universe exist?' Underneath a fragile physical shell, Hawking had an outgoing personality, and quickly understood the elements that went into making a compelling TV appearance.

CALTECH

Yet as always, advances in profession and reputation had to swim against the strong tide of ALS. Walking finally became impossible, even with crutches, and a wheelchair became a necessity. To make his life indoors easier, Caius (NB: Gonville and Caius College are often referred to simply as 'Caius') arranged a new home for him and his family in a spacious ground-floor flat on West Road in Cambridge, convenient both for access to the university premises and also for moving about the house in his wheelchair. As the 1970s progressed, his speech became less and less understandable to others (hence the BBC voice-over). In conversation with strangers, he often needed Jane or a close colleague by his side, someone who could interpret his strangled phrases. His ability to write was also in its final stages before disappearance. His signature of acceptance to the FRS took an agonizingly long time in front of an esteemed audience; when he completed his name, the room erupted in applause.

In his autobiography, Hawking admitted that Jane 'became depressed after my election' to the Royal Society. The effort of looking after the family of, now, two children, and of managing her husband's complex needs, plus the cost to her own studies and career, were all taking their toll on a dutiful and self-sacrificing woman. But change was around the corner. Hawking received an invitation from Kip Thorne at Caltech, offering him a year's visiting Fellowship in the exciting young institution. Given the state of his own body, and the pressure that relocation would put on his family, there were obvious challenges ahead, but Hawking accepted the invitation with relish.

For Jane, the move was a daunting feat of logistics, not least because out in America she wouldn't even be able to draw on the support of nearby family. One thing was certain – she could no longer cope unilaterally with Stephen's condition. She consulted doctors about next steps, but arrived at a solution that would change the practicalities of their lives: 'The idea was quite simple: we should invite Stephen's students to live with us in our large Californian house. We could offer them free accommodation in return for help with the mechanics of lifting, dressing and bathing.'[62] Here would be one of the most important decisions of Hawking's life. The first assistant chosen, one of the future many, was Bernard Carr, a graduate student working under Hawking's supervision. For the student assistants, helping Hawking with his physical challenges was by no means mere manual labour; it also gave them privileged and extended access to Hawking's assistance with their research, and additional insight into Hawking's own advanced studies.

Caltech was a literal and metaphorical breath of fresh air for Hawking. He arrived in August 1974, entering a world of sunshine, skyscrapers, accessibility (the streets were wider, flatter and laid out in more regular patterns) and an evident can-do attitude among the American academics. The standard of living was superb and the technology plentiful and advanced. An immediate pay-off for Hawking was that the university provided him free of charge with a cutting-edge electric wheelchair, which he quickly mastered.

At Caltech, Hawking was soon deeply embedded in new lines of research, aided by some of the best new American theoretical physicists, many of whom would eventually become close friends. They included not only Kip Thorne, but also revered figures such as Richard Feynman (1918–88) and Murray Gell-Mann (1929–2019). Hawking also worked closely with Caltech graduate student Don Page, together producing papers that explored further the nature and potential final demise of primordial black holes. With Jim Hartle (1939–2023), who had completed his PhD in particle physics under Gell-Mann in 1964, Hawking made further studies into the properties and behaviour of Hawking radiation, while he also co-operated with Thorne regarding the applications of general relativity to the motion of black holes. The new surroundings and the illuminating research made his year in Caltech especially stimulating.

Hawking's reputation as a physicist was not only confined to the UK and the USA, but was also spreading internationally. From across the globe there were regular invitations for Hawking to speak or to collaborate in research, and there was an increasing influx of awards and recognitions. One of the most surprising acknowledgements came in 1975. Five years previously, Hawking had been made a member of the Catholic Church's Pontifical Academy of Sciences, a notable honour given Hawking's ambiguous relationship with religion. In April 1975, however, Hawking was invited to Rome to receive none other than the Pope Pius VI Medal for distinguished work in science. In his autobiography, Hawking confesses that he considered turning down the award on principle, considering the Catholic Church's historical treatment of Galileo in the 17th century. Galileo's observations of the universe through more powerful telescopes had led to his advocacy of Copernican heliocentrism, the idea that the Earth and the other planets orbit around the Sun. This led to his being suspected of heresy (heliocentrism was contrary to Church doctrine) by the Roman Catholic Inquisition in 1633, threatened with torture, forced to recant, and condemned to spend the rest of his life under house arrest. Hawking recognized, however, that these were more modern and enlightened times, so he went to Rome to accept the medal. The trip also gave him the opportunity to visit the Vatican Library, where he was able to see Galileo's formal submission to Church doctrine of geocentrism, and to promote the idea of the Church giving a formal posthumous pardon to the great Italian scientist. After the award ceremony, Hawking also met the great physicist Paul Dirac (1902–84), who apparently confided in Hawking that he had originally advised for a different person for the papal medal, but eventually changed his mind in Hawking's favour.

THE INFORMATION PARADOX

Papal awards notwithstanding, there was plenty to do back in Caltech. While there, Hawking began to wrestle with another key issue relating to black hole physics. This was a problem known as the 'information paradox', and it was something that Hawking would explore for the next 40 years, in the process issuing some of his most provocative research.

We tend to think of the word 'information' in a fairly loose way, a generic sense of knowledge and data recorded and distributed through various different media. In physics, by contrast, the term 'information' refers to the complete set of properties and details that define the state of a system. To understand a system fully, we need to know all these properties. As an example, consider a hand-written letter. While we might consider its information to be simply the words recorded on the paper, for a physicist its information is everything that constitutes the letter as a physical system – the particles and molecules that make up the paper and ink, the structure of those particles and molecules, shape and size, etc. Important in our context here is that according to quantum mechanics, the information in the letter can be turned into a different form that is, theoretically at least, reversible. Using a common analogy, imagine taking the letter and throwing it into a fire. The letter appears completely destroyed, ultimately turned to a small pile of ash. We might therefore think that its information is irreversibly destroyed. But theoretically, if we could identify and track the history of all the letter particles and the particle behaviour of the fire, we could reverse-engineer the pile of ash, the smoke and other constituents of the process and restore them once again into an intact letter. This is because the information might have been transformed, but it is not lost. Here we come upon another inviolable law of physics – the law of information conservation. Hawking acknowledges that in physics 'information is a sacred thing', the very foundation of scientific predictability, which in turn is the foundation of most scientific laws.[63]

But Hawking began to think that when it came to the law of information conservation, black holes might prove to be the exception. They would operate under what he called the 'information paradox'. Picture all the information that falls into a black hole – particles, gases, rocks, stars, planets, spaceships, etc. If, as Hawking had argued, black holes would continually lose mass through the emission of Hawking radiation and eventually disappear, what happens to the information that went into the black hole and its singularity? Hawking began to formulate the radical idea that this information would, when the black hole finally dissipated, be lost forever. Note that he was saying that the information was *irretrievably* lost, not just hidden from view. Nor could anyone point to Hawking radiation itself as a solution; the particle emission from a specific black hole was indistinguishable from that of any other black hole, containing none of the information about the specific contents that fell into the void.

It was apparent that this theory would be challenging to many. For a start, it would threaten the sanctity of the law of information conservation. Furthermore, the possibility of absolute information loss in the universe upset the very notion of cause and effect, the model of predictability.[64]

After a year in the Californian sun, Hawking returned to Cambridge in 1975, the homecoming inducing something of a black mood after the glitz and possibilities of the USA (see page 106).

Hawking would nevertheless be a regular visitor to the USA, maintaining his ties and building connections. The country also offered some memorable stimulations. When in San Francisco, for example, Hawking became known for committing himself to wild wheelchair runs down some of the steepest streets, much to the protective terror of family and colleagues. Even confined to a wheelchair, Hawking exhibited a physically fearless streak. Indeed, throughout his life Hawking's apparent lack of regard for such inconveniences as traffic, pedestrians and obstacles would lead to numerous close calls and to some actual accidents. On 5 March 1991, for example, Hawking was actually struck by a taxi on the night-time roads in Cambridge. He was thrown and his wheelchair was destroyed, but he managed to escape with cuts, bruises and a broken arm. The accident wasn't his fault on this occasion, but it demonstrates the fact that he didn't live a physically cloistered life, however severe his condition became.

It was in San Francisco that Hawking controversially launched his idea of information loss on the world of physics. He had actually run the idea past Don Page in 1979. His friend and colleague had many reservations, but Hawking was undeterred and pushed ahead with a sense of commitment. In Kitty Ferguson's biography of Hawking, she relates how Hawking told Don Page in 1980 that 'I would rather be right than rigorous.' This was a new spirit. Hawking's intellectual abilities had already been validated. He was becoming more confident, more reckless perhaps, pushing the boundaries of science ever further.

In 1981, Hawking attended a conference held in the luxurious attic of a mansion owned by Werner Erhard, an American entrepreneur made wealthy by the delivery of mass personal development courses that were popular in the USA in the 1970s and 80s. A small group of senior physicists were present and listened patiently through Hawking's presentation. Martin Roček, who was then a junior research fellow at the DAMTP, was acting as the interpreter for the audience. As his presentation went on, Hawking explained his position on absolute information loss in black holes. He finished to the sight of perplexed faces, not knowing what to do with such an outlandish idea from such a senior figure. One scientist in particular, Leonard Susskind – a professor of physics at Stanford and a close friend of Hawking – was particularly troubled, and Hawking knew exactly why: 'We wouldn't be able to predict the future. We can't be sure of our past history either. The history books and our memories could be just illusions. It is the past that tells us who we are. Without it we lose our identity.'[65]

Thus began a long intellectual struggle between Hawking and Susskind over the information paradox, the nature of which was perfectly encapsulated in Susskind's 2008 book entitled: *The Black Hole War: My Battle with Stephen Hawking to Make the World Safe for Quantum Mechanics*.[66] It was a conflict whose front lines would not settle for decades to come.

RETURN TO THE UK

Notwithstanding his occasional visits to the USA and elsewhere, Hawking returned to Cambridge as his permanent academic base in 1975. Being back in the UK did not exactly boost his spirits. The weather was depressing and the facilities, technologies and finances in the UK seemed decades behind those in California. He also looked around and saw a culture that seemed 'restricted and parochial', and he was rattled at having to revert to a manual wheelchair after the whizzy excitement of the American electric version. The local health authority refused to provide him with a powered wheelchair, so the Hawking family had to buy one of their own at great expense.

Life in the UK, however, was becoming physically easier for the Hawking family through the use of graduate assistants to help Stephen with day-to-day living. Furthermore, as the end of Hawking's current professorship loomed, Gonville and Caius College gave him a permanent 'readership' to ensure that he stayed within the Cambridge community. This position came along with a capable secretary, Judy Fella. Don Page took over as Hawking's assistant in 1976, and together he and Judy relieved much of the pressure from Jane. It was important they did so. By this time, Hawking was becoming increasingly helpless physically; by the end of the decade he would no longer be able to feed himself.

The year 1977 brought another development in Hawking's personal life, one whose importance would increase over time. In December of that year, Jane – a person both musical and religious – joined the choir of St Mark's Church in Barton Road. There she met the recently widowed choirmaster and organist Jonathan Hellyer Jones. They quickly struck up a close friendship, finding in each other emotional repose from pressures in other parts of their lives. He became a regular visitor to the Hawking household, helping Stephen out with various practicalities, teaching Lucy piano, and playing with the children in general. Jane noted that her husband initially reacted to Jonathan 'with a certain male hostility' and tried to 'assert his intellectual superiority'. Apparently, Jonathan's generally non-competitive nature rendered him immune to these challenges.[67]

INTO THE BLACK HOLE

By the late 1970s, the friendship between Jane and Jonathan was beginning to morph into a romance. Hawking was aware of this shift, but regarded it philosophically, accepting that the likelihood of his death in the not-too-distant future meant that he could tolerate the relationship, as long as he was also the recipient of Jane's attention and love.[68]

There was much else in life claiming his attention, as his career went from strength to strength. As the 1970s played out, there was an in-rush of honorary doctorates and various awards. In 1976, for example, Hawking was awarded the Hughes Medal, granted by the Royal Society for 'outstanding research in the field of energy'. Specifically, the award was given 'For his distinguished contributions to the application of general relativity to astrophysics, especially to the behaviour of highly condensed matter.'[69]

Hawking in informal discussion with other academics in Cambridge, c. 1980.

Another accolade came in 1979, when Hawking was appointed to the Lucasian Chair of Mathematics (see page 34). Previous holders of the chair had included, as mentioned earlier, Issac Newton, as well as Charles Babbage (1791–1871) and Paul Dirac, so Hawking was in historically lofty company. He delivered his inaugural lecture to the position on 29 April 1980, his dictated text read out loud by a student. The title of the paper was a customarily provocative question: 'Are we on the verge of discovering the Theory of Everything?'

THE THEORY OF EVERYTHING

An all-encompassing, all-explaining theory of the universe was an elusive challenge built into science from its earliest history. In the domain of modern physics, the 'Grand Unified Theory' (GUT) had been a goal of physicists since the mid-1970s. Simplifying considerably, the GUT was the attempt to describe the four forces of nature (electromagnetism, gravity, the strong nuclear force and the weak nuclear force) within a single theory, so that each force would be regarded as just an aspect and expression of a single force. The closest physics had come to this was known as the 'Standard Model', a theory uniting three of the forces, but crucially excluding gravity. What Hawking referred to as the Theory of Everything was a far broader theoretical framework, uniting all aspects of the universe in an elegant and coherent explanation, including the unification of quantum mechanics and general relativity, two domains of physics with deeply entrenched differences.

In Hawking's Lucasian lecture, he raised the possibility of a Theory of Everything through the concept of '$N=8$ supergravity', obviously disappointing any members of a non-scientific audience who were hoping for some catchy philosophical soundbite. It was, he argued, a promising way of unifying quantum mechanics with general relativity's theories of gravity.

To get our heads around this proposition, we return to the basic principle that everything in the universe is composed of particles. As Hawking has explained in some of his popular works, all these particles have a property called 'spin'. This property does not refer to a rotation on an axis, but rather relates to how the particle appears when viewed from different directions. There are four types of spin, each assigned a different number:

- Spin 0 – This type of particle looks like a dot on a page, in that there is no change in its appearance whichever way you look at it.
- Spin 1 – This particle Hawking describes as like an 'arrow', in that it needs a complete revolution through 360 degrees for it to look exactly the same as it does at its starting position.
- Spin 2 – Here the particle can be represented like a 'double-headed arrow'; it looks the same if it is spun through 180 degrees. (There are, however, some small particles that look the same having turned through smaller fractions of a revolution.)
- Spin 1/2 – Somewhat counterintuitively, this particle needs to go through two complete revolutions to look the same.[70]

In *A Brief History of Time*, Hawking gives this typology some additional context: 'All the known particles in the universe can be divided into two groups: particles of spin 1/2, which make up the matter in the universe, and particles of spin 0, 1, and 2, which, as we shall see, give rise to the forces between matter particles.'[71]

With the context set, Hawking then explained how particles might fit into what he described as a 'supersymmetry' model. Supersymmetry is a theoretical framework in which every boson (a particle with integer spin) has a corresponding fermion (a particle with half-integer spin) 'superpartner', and vice versa. For example, a photon (boson) would have a superpartner called a photino (fermion), and a hypothetical gravitino (fermion) would be the superpartner of the graviton (boson). In N=8 supergravity, there are eight types of supersymmetry transformations, making it a highly symmetric theory with multiple superpartners for each particle. This model could provide a basis for developing a theory of quantum gravity and represents a significant step towards a unified Theory of Everything.

Hawking's work in supersymmetries and particle physics led in time to another one of his famous wagers, albeit a light-hearted one. Hawking found himself clashing with the theories of the British physicist Peter Higgs (1929–2024). In 1964, Higgs had proposed the existence of a new boson particle, what would come to be called the 'Higgs boson'. These were elementary particles with spin 0 that collectively formed the 'Higgs field'. What was radical about Higgs' theory was that the Higgs boson was responsible for imparting mass to other particles, a key component of the Standard Model of particle physics.

Hawking had his doubts that such a particle existed. Indeed, in 2000 he placed a bet with Gordon Kane, Professor of Physics at Michigan University, that the Higgs boson would never be found – the stake this time was a straightforward $100. As time went on, the best chance that the Higgs boson would be revealed was through the work of the Large Hadron Collider (LHC), a vastly powerful particle accelerator run by the European Organization for Nuclear Research (CERN) near Geneva. The LHC began its operations in 2009, and in July 2012 it struck gold, CERN's scientists reporting that they had indeed found evidence for the existence of the Higgs boson. Thus, Hawking conceded the bet, praising Higgs for his work and vision. Peter Higgs and his fellow researcher François Englert were awarded the Nobel Prize in Physics the following year. In 2013, however, Hawking reflected on the Higgs boson that 'physics would be far more interesting if it had not been found', stating that the LHC should move its attention now towards the exploration of supersymmetric partners for known particles.[72]

This simple wager, and the many others that Hawking took during his career, illustrates that he was, by his own admission, an inveterate scientific gambler.[73] It also shows that Hawking might well have been dogmatic and insistent at times, but he was by no means closed to change. At many points in his academic career, Hawking conceded that he was wrong, changing his mind based either on new research from others or from his own discovery of errors or conflicting answers in his own work. Hawking never regarded this as a problem, but rather intrinsic to the practice of honest science. For Hawking, science was much like the processes of natural selection within evolution, with new, strong ideas at first thriving but then dying out or transforming as mutations passed the advantage to stronger theories. His ability to shift his position without apology should be regarded as one of Hawking's professional strengths, and part of the reason for his enduring career. In the decade to come, that career would reach heights few would ever have predicted.

CHAPTER 5

NO BOUNDARIES

The 1980s was the decade that changed everything for Stephen Hawking. At the beginning of the decade, he was a highly successful theoretical physicist, prominent among the global scientific community. He also had a rising profile with the general public, but largely confined to those with an active interest in scientific affairs. By the end of the 1980s, however, he would be an international household name and a best-selling author. By that time, you would be hard-pressed to find anyone in the developed world who didn't know who Stephen Hawking was, and some of the rudiments of his work. In contrast to so many professional scientists, Hawking successfully straddled the boundary between academic and popular culture, without compromising his work in either domain. His life would never be the same again.

TROUBLE AT THE VATICAN

The early years of the 1980s again saw Hawking pushing the boundaries of science and also testing his mercurial relationship with the Vatican. Hawking had already secured the respect of the Pontifical Academy of Sciences, hence its award of the Pope Pius VI Medal six years previously. That in itself might seem surprising to us, given the long and (at times literally) torturous history of interactions between the Catholic Church and the scientific community. But in many ways the Church felt comfortable with Hawking's work. The Big Bang, for example, might have been a scientific origin story of the universe, but many theologians felt that it still left sufficient awe-inspiring room for a creator God, one who initiated the Big Bang in the first place. Also, Hawking had made some statements that, when stripped of context, seemed open to the possibility of the Christian divinity. For example, Hawking had told his biographer John Boslough that, 'The odds against a universe like ours emerging out of something like the Big Bang are enormous. I think there are clearly religious implications whenever you start to discuss the origins of the universe.'[74] *A Brief History of Time* ends with the reflection that if science managed to discover the Theory of Everything, then 'we would know the mind of God'.[75] Such sentences provided superb soundbites for people of faith.

Reintroduce context, however, and such musings are more open to non-theological interpretation. Hawking could certainly be judged as a 'spiritual' person. He was deeply inspired by the majesty and mystery of the universe. He was also careful not to criticize religion openly in public. What he said in private, of course, was another matter. In her biography, Jane Hawking explained poignantly that in the early years of their marriage they had 'fairly light-hearted' arguments about current affairs or scientific topics. Later, however, 'the damaging schism between religion and science seemed to have extended its reach into our very lives; Stephen would adamantly assert the blunt positivist stance which I found too depressing and too limiting to my view of the world'.[76]

Perhaps mirroring his personal evolution, in the later stages of his career Hawking would be far more explicit is dismissing theological explanations for the universe, showing an unhidden agnostic or atheistic stance (see Chapter 7). Yet even in the 1970s and 80s, his apparently religious pronouncements had hidden depths.

As with Einstein, to Hawking the word 'God' could be used as an imaginative shorthand for scientific purposes. In *A Brief History of Time*, Hawking did discuss God openly, but often with a sceptical inflection. He pointed out that an inflationary universe logically undermines the need for a creator. If we wind back inflation to the Big Bang, Hawking argues, we reach an origin event that has a purely physical explanation, regardless of whether you want to use God in the argument or not. Furthermore, because time itself began with the Big Bang, we can't even speak of God as its originator, as there was no 'before' in which He existed to create the universe. Hawking did speculate that God might kick-start the universe just *after* the Big Bang, to make it appear that the Big Bang was the causal provenance, but in that model the inflationary universe would 'place limits' on when God could have carried out the act of creation. The best we can say for God in *A Brief History* is that he is a central character, part of the human quest for ultimate origins.

Hawking's reflections on the divine in *A Brief History* were not yet in print when, in 1982, he was invited to speak at a cosmology conference in Rome, arranged for the Church by a Jesuit organization. In *A Brief History*, Hawking said that he was glad the Vatican was not aware of the subject of his presentation in advance. The title of his paper was 'The Boundary Conditions of the Universe', and the first sentence of the abstract was rather unthreatening: 'This paper considers the questions of what are the boundary conditions of the universe and where they should be imposed.'[77] But it contained some ideas that would be sensitive for the Vatican.

In the paper, Hawking outlined what he called the 'no-boundary condition' of the universe. This is a complex theory, related to the concept of 'imaginary time'. The visual model Hawking used to describe imaginary time was the x and y axes of a graph, the two axes meeting in the middle at 0 to form a crosshairs, with negative numbers to the left of and below the 0. The horizontal x axis represents our history in real time, from past to present going left to right. The vertical y axis, by contrast, represents 'imaginary time', a mathematical concept that allows time to be treated as a spatial dimension. The mathematics of imaginary time 'predicts not only effects we have already observed but also effects we have not been able to measure yet nevertheless believe in for other reasons'.[78] In essence, imaginary time is a mathematical tool for calculating the possible states of the universe.

In the no-boundary condition, the universe is a finite space, but one without boundaries in imaginary time, without a perimeter (a closed surface) and without a singular beginning. The 'no-boundary' part means that we could travel infinitely within the universe but never reach its end, in the same way that we could travel forever across the surface of the Earth. If we work in the standard spacetime co-ordinates (x,y,z,t) we wind up with a singularity at t=0, but a standard tool in complex analysis is to replace the variables with complex numbers. In the complex plane, singularities can be eliminated, which means that as the universe became a quantum system near the Big Bang, time vanished as a good variable to use and it was replaced by a space-like variable, and so there was no boundary (t=0) to the universe at the Big Bang itself.

The upshot of this model, Hawking argued, was that the universe requires no external intervention (i.e. God), as it would contain everything it needs, including the laws of science, to form the universe we see today.

Hawking's paper also incorporated the work of physicist Richard Feynman, who had previously developed the concept of 'sum-over-histories' (more formally, 'path integral formulation'), which provided a new framework for understanding quantum mechanics. If we consider the routes a particle can take between two points, quantum mechanics established that we can't define a singular route or velocity taken. Rather, each particle has a wide range of possible routes, 'smeared out' across the full range of probabilities. Feynman offered a mathematical model for calculating all the possible routes based on their probabilities of doing so, known as the 'amplitude'. The total probability amplitude of a particle moving from Point A to Point B is obtained by summing (adding) the contributions (amplitudes) of all these possible histories.

While sum-over-histories might sound arcane, it had importance for many domains of physics. It even raised the necessity, on a cosmological scale, of multiple universes, expressing one area of the 'many worlds' interpretation of quantum mechanics. Hawking likened the universe to a roulette wheel; just as rolling the dice contains outcomes with different probabilities but all possibilities, so with the universe. Thus, Hawking noted, 'the universe must have every possible history, each with its own probability. [...] The idea that the universe has multiple histories may sound like science fiction, but it is now accepted as science fact.'[79] This is a statement of the Hartle–Hawking wave function for the universe, which is a sum over an infinite number of possible geometric states for spacetime. It's equivalent to an electron wave function defined by the sum (superposition) of an infinite number of states.

Hawking utilized the sum-over-histories approach from 1975 onwards, feeding into his work with American theoretical physicist Jim Hartle, which in turn shaped his 1981 paper for the Vatican. Hawking explained to the audience that even a no-boundary universe wouldn't have only a single history. Instead, in imaginary time there would be an infinite number of alternate histories corresponding to every closed surface, with each historical imaginary time determining an equivalent historical real time.[80]

Underlying Hawking's Vatican paper was the 'anthropic principle', which he used to describe why the universe seems so particularly attuned to human existence. The foundation of the anthropic principle is that the very fact we observe the universe means it must have the properties necessary for our existence as observers. There are two main versions of the theory. The 'weak anthropic principle' (WAP) suggests that the universe appears the way it does simply because it is conducive to our existence; if it were different, we would not be here to see it. The 'strong anthropic principle' (SAP) posits that the universe must have the properties that necessarily lead to the emergence of intelligent life. In this model, life itself is a fundamental feature of the universe.

In Hawking's words, the anthropic principle address answers the question 'Why is the universe the way it is?' In the Vatican paper, Hawking concluded that the WAP was at work in our universe, and that while the universe therefore has the properties for intelligent life, that does not mean that intelligent life was built into the purpose of the universe. Our universe is just one of many possible universes.

Taken in aggregate, the arguments of 'The Boundary Conditions of the Universe' contained much to make the Catholic scientists and philosophers take exception. The no-boundary condition removed the need for God as a creator, the sum-over-histories could make our universe just one of many, and the WAP seemed to undermine the general possibility of human beings as divinely created creatures. After the conference, Hawking related how he met the Pope (who had not actually been present for the reading of Hawking's paper) in person. Hawking recounted how the Pope had advised scientists that they should not enquire about how the universe began, as that mystery was the province of God.[81] In 2006, press reports had Hawking repeat the claim that the Pope had attempted to warn off scientists from prying into cosmological origins. This produced counter-claims from key Catholic figures and publications. The Catholic News Agency, for example, were keen to print the actual words spoken by the pontiff back in 1981: 'Every scientific hypothesis about the origin of the world, such as the one that says that there is a basic atom from which the whole of the physical universe is derived, leaves unanswered the problem concerning the beginning of the universe. By itself science cannot resolve such a question.'[82] As we can see from these words, the Pope was not issuing a prohibition, but rather expressing his belief that the ultimate questions of our existence remain unanswered by science.

HAWKING'S BIG BANG

The theories, debates and ideas Hawking produced during the remainder of the 1980s are too numerous to cover in comprehensive detail here, but we should note one further landmark in the decade. Hawking and other DAMTP staff arranged a series of conferences sponsored by the Nuffield Foundation (an organization providing research funding), with workshops held in 1981, 1982, 1985 and 1989. The workshop that took place between 21 June and 9 July 1982 was of particular significance. This concentrated on exploring the way that galaxies and the universe as a whole formed to look the way they do. More specifically, what explained the 'perturbations' in the universe's structure?

At this time, physicist Alan Guth had proposed a theory in which the new-born universe initially underwent enormous inflation at an elevated rate of expansion, before steadying out to the rate of expansion we see today. A similar theory had already been developed by the Russian physicist Andrei Linde, whom Hawking had met at a conference in Moscow in 1980. During that conference, Hawking set about explaining what he saw as the problems in both Guth and Linde's model. What made the experience particularly agonizing for Linde was that he was actually acting as the Russian-language interpreter between Hawking's assistant (speaking for Hawking) and the conference audience, so he was essentially telling a large number of Russian physicists what was wrong with his own theories.

After the conference, however, Linde became a good friend to Hawking, and both he and Guth came to the Nuffield conference in 1982. The groundbreaking workshop looked in particular at the quantum fluctuations in the inflationary phase of the universe. Hawking also showed how a cosmological version of Hawking radiation could inform our understanding of how large-scale structures (such as galaxies) formed. Collectively, the work of the conference laid the foundations for much subsequent inflationary theory. After the conference, Hawking stated that, 'The inflationary hypothesis has the great advantage that it makes predictions about the present density of the universe and about the spectrum of departures from spatial uniformity. It should be possible to test these in the fairly near future and either falsify the hypothesis, or strengthen it.'[83]

SPEECH TO TEXT

In the same year as the 1982 Nuffield conference, Hawking celebrated his 40th birthday. For a man who had been given about two years to live 20 years earlier, evidently much remained in his favour. Honours rare in most careers kept coming at regular pace. In 1981, for instance, he received the Benjamin Franklin Medal in Physics from the Franklin Institute (a science museum and centre of science education and research in Philadelphia, Pennsylvania). At the beginning of the following year, Hawking was on the Queen's New Year's Honours list, receiving the title Commander of the British Empire. His plaudits, of course, were no defence against the incremental war being waged within his body. A turning point came in 1985.

At this stage of his intellectual journey, Hawking was doing impressive work relating to the 'arrow of time'. He began considering what would happen if universal expansion slowed, stopped, and then went into reverse. Would this mean that the thermodynamic arrow of time, i.e. entropy, would go into reverse, like clock hands being turned backwards? If so, universal disorder would decrease, not increase; the broken cup would leap from the floor and reassemble itself on the table. At first, he leaned towards this possibility. However, sceptical input from Don Page and one of Hawking's graduate students, the Canadian researcher Raymond Laflamme, demonstrated that entropy and the arrow of time would not, in fact, reverse in a contraction phase; contraction would simply turn the arrow of time in the opposite direction. Hawking, ever the honest broker, admitted his error.

In 1985, Hawking and his team, which on this trip included Laflamme, went to Switzerland, intending to spend a month at

CERN conducting research. The team now included Laura Gentry, Hawking's current secretary. Jane, Jonathan and most of the family (minus Robert) would join him in Geneva following a European campaign trip. A medical emergency, however, wrecked all plans. Jane and her group ended up rushing to Geneva after Gentry phoned, informing her that Hawking had been hospitalized with pneumonia and that his situation was life-threatening. At the hospital, senior doctors presented Jane with a blunt choice: she could turn off her husband's life-support system, resulting in his death, or they could attempt to save him, but this would involve giving him a tracheotomy. Even that might not save him, but if it did, he would forever be compelled to breathe through a throat tube. Furthermore, he would never speak again.

With foresight and bravery, Jane opted for the operation, although this was conducted by specialists back at Addenbrooke's Hospital, Cambridge. Throughout his adult life, Hawking would have numerous near misses with death. Most, however, demonstrated Hawking's remarkable abilities for recovery. The episode in 1985, though, had a profound impact. From this point on, Hawking would essentially need 24-hour nursing care (especially to ensure that he was breathing properly), a service beyond regular National Health Service (NHS) provision and also beyond the family finances. Hawking had also now lost a key element of control. No longer could he make even basic vocalizations; the only way he could communicate was for someone to hold up a card with the letters of the alphabet, point to them in turn, and Hawking raise his eyebrows when the right letter was indicated.

Thankfully, the financial mountain was at least temporarily scaled through funding from the John D. and Catherine T.

MacArthur Foundation (shortened to 'MacArthur Foundation'), a US organization that invested in important scientific research. Now the Hawkings could hire care staff in volume and expertise, capable of looking after Stephen's major physical needs. One particularly significant hire was Elaine Mason, a strident and vibrant nurse whose spirit and energy meant she quickly connected with her new patient. She would thereafter become Hawking's right-hand person and, in time, much more.

A solution to Hawking's speech came via some technological angels. The first of these was Walter (Walt) Woltosz, an American aerospace engineering graduate and the founder of Words Plus Inc., a developer and manufacturer of computer-based communication systems. Walt, along with his wife Ginger, had designed a specific solution for Ginger's mother, Lucille Evans, who had also suffered from ALS. The system was called 'Equalizer' and when told by third parties about Hawking's condition they graciously donated one of the machines.

Equalizer was basically a computer interface in which the user, through minimal hand movements, selected words from a menu of about 2,500 options, the words predictively organized to aid logical efficiency in selection. When the user saw the right word, they clicked it, which then passed them to various sub-menus, until the sentence was complete. When the text was ready, the user could then activate the computer's synthetic voice to speak the words out loud. The whole business, compared to regular speech or typing, remained achingly slow – about three words a minute – but it worked. For Hawking, this piece of liberating hardware and software was significantly enhanced by David Mason, Elaine's husband and a computer engineer. He fitted the whole device to the arm of Hawking's wheelchair and installed a special adaptive clicker. Now Hawking could take his communication system with him. With practice, his proficiency in using it also increased – on occasions he could produce about 15 words per minute.

Equalizer threw Hawking a lifeline. Now he could still, with significant adaptation and support, lecture, speak and interact, albeit with heavy time-lag or through pre-recorded messages. He also, crucially, settled on a particular voice from the computer's options. This voice, with a hint of a US accent, would be the one we associated with Stephen Hawking until the very end of his life, despite more polished voices arising as technology improved. He felt that it was *his* voice, a fundamental expression of his identity. In his autobiography, he explained that the voice 'has become my trademark, so I won't change it for a more natural-sounding voice unless all three [remaining] synthesizers break'.[84]

EXPANSION

Equalizer delivered one particular benefit that was to define Hawking's academic and financial future: it enabled him to write books.

University researchers, scholars and professors are expected to publish their research at regular points during their careers. But for the most part, the publications are papers and articles published in specialist journals, with the occasional foray into a full-scale scientific book offered by an academic publisher. In the 1980s, however, Hawking's vision for scientific publishing went well beyond those limits. Hawking was driven by the urge to share the highest-level scientific thinking with the broadest possible audience, a goal many would regard as an exercise in futility. In a pure academic setting, Hawking could let fly with his full scientific and mathematical arsenal, leaving behind those who couldn't keep up. But he also showed no snobbery towards the general public. Transferring elite knowledge to common understanding was to him both important and worthy, and Hawking also seemed to regard it as an intellectual challenge few could meet. At base level, he wanted the world to enjoy science.

If we put aside Hawking's dozens of journal articles, he published his first full-length book in the 1970s, *The Large Scale Structure of Space-Time*, co-authored with mathematician George Ellis and published by Cambridge University Press (CUP). It was a treatise on general relativity and its applications to cosmology, explaining the collaborative work Hawking had undertaken with Penrose and others. It was emphatically *not* for the general reader. In fact, according to Hawking's later honest appraisal, the book was inaccessible to most scientists too, 'unreadable' for anyone except a well-informed theoretical physicist. In the 1980s, however, Hawking shifted his position. He looked instead to write a *popular* book in theoretical physics and cosmology, one intended for any interested reader, even those with no scientific background. To be digestible, therefore, it had to exclude mathematics, the soil in which physics grows. It was a challenging brief to himself.

Hawking said later that there was, in part, a financial imperative behind his decision to write the book – he needed to find money to pay Lucy's school fees.[85] The remuneration would also help with his long list of care costs. Only by concentrating on the mass market might he see a significant return on his investment; academic works rarely sold more than a few thousand copies.

By contrast, Hawking wanted his book everywhere – high-street bookshops, airports, book clubs.

He just had to find a publisher. His first choice was naturally CUP, already receptive to his work. The world's oldest university press was, however, sniffy at the idea of a popular science work. They felt a more heavyweight title was appropriate, with expectations that it might sell about 20,000 copies. Such figures were mighty for most academic titles, but Hawking wanted to see far higher sales. He recruited a literary agent, Al Zuckerman, to help expedite the process, and gave him a first draft of the book in 1984. Given Hawking's physical struggles (which would only get worse after the health crisis the following year), just to get the initial manuscript together was a work of Herculean labour. By Hawking's own account, Zuckerman also leaned towards targeting the book at a more specialist audience, and recommended placing it with W.W. Norton and Co., a prestigious New York publisher with a long back catalogue of professional and academic titles. Hawking remained obdurate about his mission, however, and eventually he opted for a quite different US publisher, Bantam. They were a true mass-market bookseller, with particularly strong access to airport bookshops. While several other publishers turned the book down, seeing it as sitting awkwardly between academic and popular markets, Bantam's commissioning editors saw its potential sales to aspirational, educated readers wanting a deep-dive into the greatest questions of the universe. Hawking's reputation was already high, and he was paid $250,000 for the US rights (from Bantam-Transworld) and £30,000 for the British rights.[86]

Now he just had to finish writing the book, using the Equalizer system. Getting the reading level right was imperative. Hawking was assigned an uncompromising editor at Bantam, Peter Guzzardi, who scrutinized each manuscript chapter critically and asked for copious changes. (It helped that Guzzardi was a non-scientist, so if he didn't understand what Hawking was saying, it was likely the reader wouldn't either.) The book's focus on the mass market was unchanged, but it would also be a demanding work, requiring slow reading and considered thought.

The book that emerged also says something about the way that Hawking thought. Hawking has described how the loss of speech and writing meant that he not only learned how to do and hold all the mathematics in his head, but that he also developed a particularly strong capacity for visual thinking. This skill in turn made Hawking adept at moulding complex theoretical concepts into relatable real-world analogies, which would prove invaluable to take the intimidation factor out of his book. In this effort, he was also assisted by his then graduate assistant, Brian Whitt, who at that time was working on his PhD, 'Gravity: A quantum theory?' Whitt's diligent support also helped to speed up the pace of production.

The working title of Hawking's book was *From the Big Bang to Black Holes: A Short History of Time*. With that canny publisher's eye for subtle title tweaks, Guzzardi changed the word *Short* to *Brief*. Finally, the manuscript went from draft to final version, then through copyediting, typesetting and print. Publication was scheduled for spring 1988, by which time expectation was already stirring in the popular press. On 8 February 1988, for example, *Time* magazine carried a lengthy profile of Hawking. It included an observant comment from one of Hawking's colleagues that chimes with points made previously:

Hawking's ability to perceive complex truths without doodling long equations on paper astounds his colleagues. 'He has an ability to visualize four-dimensional geometry that is almost unique,' says Werner Israel, a University of Alberta physicist who has collaborated with Hawking in relating mini-black holes to the new cosmic-string theories. Observes Kolb: 'It's like Michael Jordan playing basketball. No one can tell Jordan what moves to make. It's intuition. It's feeling. Hawking has a remarkable amount of intuition.'[87]

Also in the article, Hawking made a comment on the accessibility of the book for the public that is often quoted: 'Someone told me that each equation I included in the book would halve the sales,' says Hawking. 'In the end, however, I did put in Einstein's famous equation $E = mc^2$. I hope that this will not scare off half my potential readers.'[88]

Publication was imminent, expectations were high. But there was a last-minute drama. A review copy of the book was sent to Don Page, and the verdict was not good. Page found numerous errors, particularly in the text related to illustrated content. Bantam had to face the pain of pulling the printed copies and shredding them, while embarking on a frantic three weeks of making corrections and reprinting. But finally, *A Brief History of Time* was published on 1 April 1988.

A Brief History of Time was, and remains, one of the most influential achievements in modern scientific writing, a sweeping exploration of cosmology and theoretical physics across 12 intense chapters, showcasing Hawking's insights and interpretations. It also carried an introduction by the great science writer Carl

Sagan, although for copyright reasons that introduction was removed after the first edition. The breadth of topics in the book was impressive, from special and general relativity to light cones and black hole radiation, and from quantum mechanics and singularities to particle spin and the anthropic principle. All these topics were unified in Hawking's quest for answers to life's greatest questions, but also by his wry humour and irreverence. Publishers, and the literary world, watched with expectation to see whether the book would fly off the shelves or sit there gathering dust.

A Brief History of Time *made Hawking an academic superstar.*

As history subsequently showed, sales exceeded the very highest expectations, not just for the first months but for the years to come. In a foreword to a later (2015) edition, Hawking provided some data: the book was on the *New York Times* bestseller list for 147 weeks; it was on the London *Sunday Times* bestseller list for a record 237 weeks; it has been translated into more than 40 languages; more than ten million copies have been sold. In many ways, *A Brief History of Time* helped to give birth to the popular science category that is so voluminous today; it proved there was an appetite for widespread scientific knowledge.

NO BOUNDARIES

In *My Brief History*, Hawking devotes considerable length (in such a short book) to reflecting on the success of *A Brief History of Time*. Not only did the book make Hawking a millionaire, but it also put his career into escape velocity, breaking through the boundaries between science and popular culture. He discusses some of the press reviews at the time, and noted a certain formula, respecting the work but also playing on the 'human interest angle' regarding his ALS.[89] He showed the self-awareness to acknowledge that his illness had, to a significant degree, helped fuel the publicity for his book. But he fended off accusations that Bantam were exploiting his illness by featuring a photograph of him on the cover. He also gave riposte to those who scorned what they saw as the intellectual pretensions of the readers, saying that many bought the book, but few actually read it. As an aside, in 2014 the American mathematician and blogger Jordan Ellenberg invented what he called the 'Hawking Index', a mathematical measure of how far people will actually read into a challenging book before giving up. (Its algorithm was based upon the popular highlights feature used in Kindle, specifically how far the average highlights reached into the book.)

Hawking responded by pointing to the fact that from the moment *A Brief History of Time* was published, he came under an avalanche of correspondence from interested readers with follow-up questions, and was regularly approached by enthusiasts in the street. There remains a humorous debate about the public's handling of this admittedly difficult book. It is widely referred to as 'the most unread book of all time', but at the same time features on *Time* magazine's 'All-*TIME* 100 Best Non-Fiction Books' (it sits very respectably at no. 16).

NO BOUNDARIES

A Brief History of Time was the beginning of Hawking's exceptional literary career. The book alone went into several editions, including with updated chapters and new visuals. Seeing the public appetite for his work, in 1993 Hawking published *Black Holes and Baby Universes and Other Essays*. As the title suggests, this was a collection of Hawking's important essays and lectures, but it also included some of his reflections on his early life, plus an interview with the author. In 1996, Hawking published a book with his long-time collaborator, Roger Penrose, called *The Nature of Space and Time*, which recorded the debates between the two scientists on key issues in theoretical physics and cosmology, including the possibility of uniting quantum theory of fields and Einstein's general theory of relativity and the conclusions about the information-loss paradox in black holes. The following year, Hawking, along with philosophers of science Abner Shimony and Nancy Cartwright, contributed critical analysis to Penrose's work *The Large, the Small and the Human Mind*, an attempt to formulate a holistic vision of the universe, including the contribution made by the human mind.

Hawking's next solo book hit the shelves in 2001. *The Universe in a Nutshell* was essentially a heavyweight extension of *A Brief History of Time*, including up-to-date thinking on topics such as string theory and branes (see next chapter). It was also well received, winning the Aventis Prize for Science Books in 2002.

Other works followed thick and fast, demonstrating how productively Hawking settled into the publishing groove. In 2002, Running Press published *On the Shoulders of Giants: The Great Works of Physics and Astronomy*, a collection of landmark historical scientific texts, to which Hawking provided both an introduction and a commentary. That same year came Hawking's *The Future of Spacetime,* co-authored with Kip Thorne, Igor Novikov, Timothy Ferris and with an introduction by Alan Lightman. In 2005, Hawking put his name to another anthology, this time bringing together seminal works of mathematics: *God Created the Integers: The Mathematical Breakthroughs That Changed History.* He also published *A Briefer History of Time,* a more compact version of his classic with some simplified sections and new content, written with the US theoretical physicist and mathematician Leonard Mlodinow, who would become a significant collaborator on Hawking's published work in the 2000s. From 2007, as mentioned in Chapter 3, Hawking also diversified into children's publishing, assisting his daughter Lucy and the French physicist Christophe Galfard to write a science-based adventure story, *George's Secret Key to the Universe.* This went on to achieve enormous international success, spawning five more books in the series, all of which received Hawking's input.

Hawking's next major work was co-authored with Mlodinow. *The Grand Design: New Answers to the Ultimate Questions of Life* was an important work, which we will study in the final chapter, in which Hawking sought to bring together as complete a Theory of Everything as he could muster, generating some interesting controversies in the process. *The Dreams That Stuff Is Made Of: The Most Astounding Papers of Quantum Physics and How They Shook the Scientific World*, a compilation of essential writings in physics selected by Hawking, followed in 2011.

In 2013, Hawking made a distinct departure in his publishing focus with the short autobiography, *My Brief History.* It was a witty, sharp and warm self-portrait, restrained in revealing many

NO BOUNDARIES

details (especially those that would expose family members) and revealing in others. It also formed a useful anchor point for information, providing some reliability among a mass of press reporting about his life.

Hawking's final work, *Brief Answers to the Big Questions*, was a fitting end to Hawking's career as a writer. It collected an important range of Hawking's essays and articles to answer ten foundational questions, including 'Is there a God?', 'Can we predict the future?', 'Is time travel possible?' and 'How do we shape the future?' The book was published in October 2018, seven months after Hawking had died. Illustrious colleagues and family ensured that the book was completed; the foreword was written by the actor Eddie Redmayne and an introduction was provided by Kip Thorne. It also included a beautifully tender afterword by Lucy Hawking. Reviews of this work were heartfelt and recognized its

A view of Hawking's speech synthesizer computer menu, as developed by the late 1990s.

importance. The Brazilian physicist and astronomer Marcelo Gleiser said of the author and the book: 'Stephen Hawking is one of those rare luminaries whose life symbolizes the best humanity has to offer ... [this is a book] every thinking person worried about humanity's future should read.'[90]

This brisk overview of Hawking's publishing career demonstrates that he was every bit as much a writer as a thinker. The two might seem synonymous, but they represent quite different skills, especially for an academic attempting to reach a general audience. Hawking's talent as an author was his ability to express and package very difficult concepts in plain language. But he was also unafraid of stretching the reader's intellectual abilities, often to the limit. Hawking's readers always feel respected.

Hawking arrived at the end of the 1980s a genuine scientific superstar. The awards and accolades kept rushing in. They included, in 1989, being named to the Order of the Companions of Honour by Her Majesty Queen Elizabeth II, someone he would meet on several occasions. He also received five honorary degrees in the 1980s, including one from his own university, Cambridge, the latter an almost unheard-of occurrence. A *Newsweek* cover strapline from 1988 perhaps summed up Hawking's status most pithily: 'Master of the Universe'. The opening paragraph of the corresponding article perfectly captures the public fascination with Hawking at that time:

> Like light from a collapsing star, exhausted by the struggle against gravity, the thoughts of Stephen Hawking reach us as if from a vast distance, a quantum at a time. Unable to speak, paralyzed by a progressive, incurable disease, the 46-year-old British physicist

communicates with the world by a barely perceptible twitch of his fingers, generating one computer-synthesized word approximately every six seconds, consuming an entire day in composing a 10-page lecture. And the world awaits the words, for the same reason that astronomers search the heavens for the precious photons from remote galaxies, or that Newton spent his last years consumed by Biblical prophecy: Hawking is trying to read the mind of God.[91]

The 'Master of the Universe' descriptor was also the title of a 30-minute BBC2 TV special broadcast in December 1989, giving a brief insight into Hawking's life and work.

If anyone predicted that Hawking's success had peaked in the 1980s, however, they would be confounded in the decade to come.

CHAPTER 6

WORMS, STRINGS AND PEAS

The 1990s was a decade in which Hawking's celebrity rose to something of a frenzy. The word 'celebrity' is a curious one to apply to a scientist, but in Hawking's case it was justified. His global public profile came to rival that of a Hollywood A-lister. His life became a whirlwind of travel, lectures, interviews, TV appearances, book launches, documentaries, conferences and high-powered meetings. Such energy was testament to his brilliance and his work ethic, which remained unrelenting. It was almost inevitable, however, that the heat of the spotlight would leave some burn marks on his personal life. The changes in the 1990s were, therefore, both painful and significant. But regardless of the ebb and flow of his personal life, the science remained central.

WORMHOLES AND BABY UNIVERSES

As outlined in the previous chapter, in 1996, Bantam Press issued a new edition of *A Brief History of Time*. Given that the first edition had been published eight years previously, and that Hawking's theories had advanced since then, the time was right to update his famous book. Thus Hawking added a new chapter and other additional content, reflecting some of his new lines of thought. The new chapter was headed 'Wormholes and Time Travel' – Hawking always had a knack for a title that would instantly snap to public interest.

WORMS, STRINGS AND PEAS

The concept of wormholes was well established by 1996. In 1935, Albert Einstein and the American-Israeli physicist Nathan Rosen (1909–95) had worked together furthering the implications of Einstein's general relativity. Together they produced the theory of the 'Einstein–Rosen bridge'. The bridge in question existed in spacetime, in which two distant locations in the universe are connected by a thin tube of spacetime. This tube provides a spatial and temporal shortcut between the two points. As an analogy (similar to that used by Hawking), imagine a long sheet of paper with 'Point A' written at one end and 'Point B' at the other. The two points are separated by the measurable length of the paper. Now bend the paper so that it forms a curved C-shape, with the ends of the sheet close together. Now Points A and B are still on the same position on the paper, but are much closer to each other on the vertical measurement. Take a drinking straw and push it through the paper to connect Point A and Point B – the straw is the Einstein–Rosen bridge.

If you now think of Point A representing our Earth and Point B representing Proxima Centauri (the closest star to Earth, 4.24 light-years away), you will understand the cosmic potential of the bridge. Before people could jump at the possibility of a fast-track route to other galaxies, Einstein and Rosen pointed out some of the issues. For example, the bridge would be open for a fantastical fraction of a second, quickly pinching out to form two singularities. Not exactly a practical route of travel. But the Einstein–Rosen bridge would go on to be influential in theoretical physics and cosmology, albeit with a catchier name bestowed by Wheeler – the 'wormhole'.

Hawking began exploring the mathematics and theories of wormholes more deeply in the late 1980s. In the new edition of *A*

Brief History of Time, he looked directly at the theoretical models of wormholes as possible apertures for time travel. First, Hawking disregarded some science-based fantasies of time travel. This included faster-than-light travel (sorry, fans of the *Millennium Falcon* spaceship in *Star Wars*), which would enable the voyager to go from Event A to Event B, arriving at B before A had even started. As we have already seen, there are some strict physical laws preventing speeds beyond that of light.

So, Hawking reflected on whether it was possible for 'an advanced civilization to keep a wormhole open', and use that as the mode of transit across time and space.[92] He demonstrated that, on a theoretical level, it might be feasible if such a civilization could create a region of spacetime with negative curvature, which he likened to the surface of a saddle, rather than positive curvature, which is like the shape of a sphere. They would do so via the Casimir effect, where a negative energy density is created between two metal plates that allow only virtual particle pairs of certain resonant wavelengths to exist between them.[93] This results in an energy density between the plates that is less than the surrounding space, illustrating how quantum mechanics might permit negative energy, which is speculated to warp spacetime and potentially stabilize a wormhole. However, Hawking noted that such effects are extremely small and remain purely theoretical in the context of creating usable wormholes.

But the *possibility* of wormholes was there, and Hawking connected that possibility to another of his intriguing ideas, that of 'baby universes'. This he began formulating in the 1980s and explained more in his 1993 work *Black Holes and Baby Universes and Other Essays*. To visualize the basic theory, imagine our universe as a child's balloon. Now picture that the balloon has a tiny imperfection in its rubber surface, one that causes a small section to inflate outwards from the wide surface, like a conjoined bubble. As it expands, it creates something like a separate, miniature balloon, still attached to the host balloon by what has become a thin rubber tube. The balloon offshoot is now our 'baby universe'.

Hawking argued that this model was possible on a cosmological scale. Quantum fluctuations in the universe could cause tiny regions of space to inflate into enormous but separate regions of spacetime. These baby universes would be universes in their own right, but still connected to ours by a tiny quantum wormhole. Hawking theorized that our own universe could have spawned many, many baby universes, birthed from tiny points of reality all around us, forming universes hidden from our view. New wormholes between these universes would form and die constantly. But again, Hawking reined in our excitement, pointing out that as the wormholes would be just 10^{-33}cm across, and would again disappear with astounding brevity, their utility as portals for quick trips to other dimensions was essentially zero.

TIME TRAVEL

The possibilities for practical time travel were, according to Hawking, not encouraging. To the list of theoretical objections he added evidentiary and philosophical problems. Jumping ahead to 2010, Hawking was in that year the centrepiece of a major three-part television documentary series, broadcast in Britain as *Stephen Hawking's Universe* (in the USA it was *Into the Universe with Stephen Hawking*). Episode 2 of the series was entitled 'Time Travel'. In one scene, Stephen Hawking sat in a lavishly decorated hall, a celebratory table replete with bowls of food and plenty of champagne. A banner hung across the room: 'Welcome Time Travellers'. The invitations printed for the event gave more context:

> You are cordially invited to a reception for Time Travellers.
> Hosted by Professor Stephen Hawking.
>
> To be held at
> The University of Cambridge
> Gonville and Caius College
> Trinity Street
> Cambridge
>
> Location: 52° 12' 21" N, 0° 7' 4.7" E
> Time: 12:00 UT 06/28/2009
> No RSVP required

In his voice-over, Hawking explained that none of these invitations would be given out before the event. Instead, the hope was that some of the copies would survive for hundreds, perhaps thousands, of years after the event, by which moment in history time travel would have become possible and visitors from the future would attend. The party, however, remained a solitary affair.

Back to *A Brief History of Time*, and Hawking gets philosophical about time travel, noting that in our present world we see no indications of visitors from other, distant periods in history. Why? A simple explanation offered is that we have already seen the past, and the fact that it remains fixed means that the spacetime warping necessary to travel back to it does not exist. That does, however, not necessarily preclude the possibility of *future* time being visited by time travellers. Hawking also addresses some of the seminal paradoxes of time travel, such as what would happen to us if we travelled back in time and killed our grandfather? But Hawking offers 'two possible resolutions' to this paradox. The first he labels the 'consistent histories approach'. In this theory, even if time travel is possible, it might be that the actions taken across spacetime must nevertheless remain consistent with the laws of physics. Thus a time traveller to the past would have to remain a passive observer, not performing actions that could affect the path of his future/present self. This position was reflecting what Hawking previously called, in a 1992 paper, the 'chronology protection conjecture'. This stated that the laws of physics prevent macroscopic bodies (i.e. those visible to the naked eye) from transporting information back into the past.[94]

A different, more intriguing, option was the 'alternative histories solution'. In this case, the time traveller who goes back into the past essentially enters a new history, different from the recorded history. Because that history is now different, because of the new present moment, he is free to act within that past. Now the original line of history no longer exists for the time traveller, but a new line of history is created. Thus time comes to have distinct junctions in which many possible alternative histories are viable.

Hawking's discussion of time travel was not frothy sci-fi fun. He connected the alternative histories solution to Feynman's sum-over-histories, another theory in which time can take many possible different routes. Given that, in *The Universe in a Nutshell* he reflects: 'If one applies the Feynman sum-over-histories to a particle, one has to include histories in which the particle travels faster than light and even backward in time.'[95] In *A Brief History of Time*, Hawking also discusses how an antiparticle falling into a black hole can be regarded as a particle 'traveling backward in time out of the hole'.[96]

(As a side note to black holes, in the early 1990s Hawking used further data collected about the CMBR to propose that the early universe might have had an event horizon, and that thermal radiation from this could have caused the density fluctuations in spacetime that caused celestial bodies to appear. Later observational evidence seemed to confirm this theory.)[97]

All this led to the question: 'Does quantum theory allow time travel on a macroscopic scale, which people could use?'[98] He suggested not. The chronology protection conjecture, like the cosmic censorship conjecture, 'has not been proved but there are reasons to believe it is true'.[99]

STRINGS AND SUPERSTRINGS

Another subject into which Hawking was drawn in the 1990s was string theory, which in due course became another candidate for a Theory of Everything. String theory was first formulated in the 1960s and 70s by the likes of Gabriele Veneziano, Leonard Susskind, Yoichiro Nambu and Holger Bech Nielsen. The core idea within string theory was that the fundamental building blocks of the universe were not point-like particles, but rather one-dimensional strings. They might have open ends like a cut piece of string, or they might form loops. The strings vibrate with contrasting wavelengths and frequencies; the specific wavelength corresponds with the properties of different fundamental particles. In string theory, what we regard as the emission or absorption of one particle by another is caused by the strings dividing or joining.[100]

String theory principally attempted to explain aspects of the nuclear force binding together protons and neutrons in the nuclei of atoms, but over time it went far beyond those parameters and became a possible unified theory for all fundamental forces, including gravity. It also had a mind-bending relationship to time and space. Hawking points out in *A Brief History* that whereas a particle occupies a single point in space at a single moment in time, a string 'occupies a line in space at each moment in time'.[101] Thus whereas a particle can be represented by a line in spacetime (its 'worldline'), a string's history is a 'two-dimensional surface called the world-sheet', with any point on the world-sheet described by two numbers, one specifying time and the other the position of a specific point on the string.[102]

String theory is conceptually demanding, and it quickly gets weirder, at least to non-scientists. Because of their mathematical properties, strings exist in more than the familiar four dimensions. Different versions of string theory therefore vary in the number of dimensions they require; some go as high as 26! These theories get around the inherent strangeness of their multiple dimensions by positing that the dimensions beyond our traditional four can be curled over or folded up on themselves, resulting in the extra dimensions being compacted to an extent beyond which we can detect them. The classic representation of this model is to think of such a dimension as like a string – it has length, circumference and diameter, but viewed from a distance it appears as a flat line, devoid of dimensions.

WORMS, STRINGS AND PEAS

String theory created as many theoretical problems as it solved. One way of addressing some of these problems was the development of supersymmetry, the theory that suggests each fermion has a boson superpartner and vice versa (see page 111). Superstring theory, which is a major advancement beyond the original string theory, essentially combines string theory with supersymmetry. Superstring theory requires a total of ten dimensions, with six of them being curled up to very small scales. The intention was to make the mathematical models of string theory more consistent and to incorporate gravity in a way that aligned with quantum mechanics.

Superstring theory encompasses five different consistent versions or sub-theories: Type I, Type IIA, Type IIB, heterotic-O (HO) and heterotic-E (HE). Each of these theories describes different types of strings and their interactions, including how strings vibrate and the symmetries they obey. The theory also received an additional theoretical layer from DAMTP staff member Paul Townsend, who, as described by Hawking, 'realized that strings are just one member of a wide class of objects that can be extended in more than one dimension'.[103] These objects he called 'p-branes', and they represented superstring objects with any number of spatial dimensions. Hawking provides more detail on this confusing mental image, first starting with the fact that the 'p' denotes the number of dimensions involved. A '0-brane' is a point-like particle, and a '1-brane' is a particle in the shape of a string (as in superstring theory; in fact, superstrings are classified as p = 1). A '2-brane' is a two-dimensional surface, like a sheet or membrane. Beyond this we begin climbing into '3-brane', '4-brane' etc., the number representing the number of dimensions involved. Like superstrings, the

WORMS, STRINGS AND PEAS

p-branes have a tension and energy in their properties, and they can also cross spacetime.

The full scope of Hawking's theoretical relationship to strings, superstrings and p-branes is beyond the scope of what we can cover here (the reader should here consult *The Universe in a Nutshell*, Chapter 7, for more details). Suffice to say, however, Hawking saw immense promise in superstrings and related theories for the discovery of a Theory of Everything.

From the mid-1990s, the possibility of finding the Theory of Everything seemed to inch closer in what was called 'M-theory'. This was not a singular theory in itself, but rather a unification of the five dominant superstring theories plus the theory of 11-dimensional supergravity into a single theoretical framework. The concept of 'supergravity' was formulated back in the late 1970s by the physicists Eugène Cremmer (1942–2019), Bernard Julia (1952–) and Joël Scherk (1946–80). We are already familiar with the theory of supersymmetry (the symmetrical relationship between bosons and fermions) and with the gravitational theory of general relativity. Supergravity was essentially the combination of both, but extending the quantum dimension of gravity by adding a gravitino (the fermion of gravity) as a superparticle to the graviton boson, the particle that mediates gravity. It was thus a theory of gravity that included quantum mechanics. The 11 dimensions in its descriptor are the maximum number of dimensions allowed by a single supersymmetry, that is, a symmetry that doesn't then break up into multiple symmetries or which causes theoretical problems like infinities, where the values calculated become infinitely large or small, which often indicates a breakdown in the integrity of theory. The 11 dimensions are, specifically, 10 spatial dimensions and 1 time dimension.

It was M-theory, particularly when p-branes were incorporated, that Hawking came to regard as the most promising candidate for the Theory of Everything. (M-theory itself was first conjectured by the American theoretical physicist Edward Witten in 1995.) In *The Universe in a Nutshell*, in the last chapter titled 'Brane New World', Hawking likened M-theory to a jigsaw that was complete to some depth around its edges, but was unfinished in the middle. He admitted that 'there is still a gaping hole at the center of the M-theory jigsaw where we don't know what is going on. We can't really claim to have found the Theory of Everything until we have filled that hole.'[104] It was filling that hole to which he would direct much effort for the last two years of his life.

HOLOGRAPHS AND DARK MATTER

There were many other domains of theoretical physics and cosmology that received Hawking's attention during the 1990s, far more than we can explore comprehensively here. For example, Hawking extended research into what is called the 'holographic principle', which had been developed by Dutch theoretical physicist Gerard 't Hooft as a potential solution to black hole information loss. It was later refined by Leonard Susskind, who applied it to string theory and quantum gravity to explain how a lower-dimensional boundary could encode all the information about the higher-dimensional volume. Its core principle was that all the information that was contained in a certain volume of space could be represented by a theory on the boundary of that space. Think of this in terms of a hologram. A hologram is created by taking the information in a two-dimensional image and using it to create a corresponding three-dimensional image. The two-dimensional image, therefore, represents a kind of flat information boundary to the three-dimensional space.

Hawking extended the holographic principle into important theoretical domains, including the information loss paradox, seeing the information of the black hole 'smeared' across a two-dimensional event horizon. This was important, because it saw Hawking turning back from his previous theories of absolute information loss within a black hole singularity. He also pointed to the broader implications of the holographic principle for quantum gravity and the very nature of spacetime. Was it possible, he asked, that there could be a two-dimensional 'cosmic horizon' out there at the edge of space, from which our three-dimensional universe was a projection?

The holographic principle would be another theory underwriting Hawking's work through the 1990s and into the new millennium, making a key appearance in one of his last papers before his death. During this decade, Hawking is clearly straining towards a Theory of Everything with every conceptual and theoretical muscle. One further step forward came with his ideation of the 'brane world', explained in *The Universe in a Nutshell*. (Admittedly, this is one of the more complex parts of the book, so careful and slow reading in the original is essential to gain the full breadth of the theory.)

We should remember that a brane (derived from the word 'membrane') is a theoretical object that exists in multiple dimensions. Hawking's brane world consists of a four-dimensional space – i.e. our universe – contained within a higher-dimensional spacetime. The latter can propagate between multiple brane worlds that exist in proximity to each other. Brane worlds can be close – very close – to one another; our own universal brane world might be just millimetres from another. But we can't see that other dimension, because light is confined within the branes. Gravity, however, exists in higher-dimensional spacetime, so its effects can spread between brane worlds; so we in our universe would feel the gravitational effects from a nearby 'shadow brane'. Hawking explains that, 'In our brane such gravitational forces would appear to be produced by sources that were truly "dark" in that the only way we could detect them is through their gravity.'[105]

As this sentence hints, Hawking offers the theory of brane worlds as a potential solution to the scientific quest to discover the 'dark matter' of the universe. Dark matter, as a concept, dates back to the 19th century in its earliest manifestations, but its presence, or not, became a theoretical challenge during the second half of the 20th century. It is offered as an answer to a mathematical problem detected in cosmological observations. Specifically, the rotational velocities of stars in spiral galaxies suggests that there is actually not enough observable matter in the outer parts of the spiral to provide the gravity that would keep the galaxy from flying apart. Therefore, there must be some other source of mass holding the galaxy together, and this unobservable force is labelled 'dark matter'. CERN explains more about this mysterious property, and its fundamental relationship to the structure of the universe:

> Unlike normal matter, dark matter does not interact with the electromagnetic force. This means it does not absorb, reflect or emit light, making it extremely hard to spot. In fact, researchers have been able to infer the existence of dark matter only from the gravitational effect it seems to have on visible matter. Dark matter

seems to outweigh visible matter roughly six to one, making up about 27% of the universe.[106]

Hawking used his brane-world theory as a potential explanation of this prevalent dark matter. Dark matter could be interpreted as the gravitational force of one brane world providing additional gravitational effect in another brane world.

Brane worlds are just one of Hawking's contributions to the possible construction of all that exists. In *The Universe in a Nutshell*, Hawking tests out the many possibilities of brane-world theory, including reflecting on how they might contribute towards explaining the inflationary expansion of the universe. He also combines the brane world with holography to suggest a radically different potential relationship between humanity and reality: 'So maybe we think we live in a four-dimensional world because we are shadows cast on the brane by what is happening in the interior of the bubble [the spherical brane world].'[107]

Inflationary models of the universe were an ongoing cause of debate during the 1990s and the 2000s, and Hawking naturally found himself in the thick of the action. He, and mathematical physicist Neil Turok, contributed another, controversial, element with a curious title: the 'pea instanton'.

The problem Hawking faced was that many models of universal inflation were not compatible with his and Hartle's no-boundary proposal. The no-boundary proposal implied that the universe would eventually contract back in on itself in the Big Crunch, but a 1995 paper from Turok, Martin Bucher and Alfred Goldhaber at Stony Brook University, New York suggested an open universe, undergoing infinite inflation.

WORMS, STRINGS AND PEAS

Turok and Hawking consulted over ways in which their respective models might be harmonized, and arrived at the vision of the 'instanton' as an explanation for how the universe we know could have transitioned from a quantum state. The instanton is an irregular four-dimensional sphere about the mass of a pea, although greatly smaller. This sphere contains all spacetime, and underwent a massive, sudden inflation to create the universe we see today, without the need for a singularity or a 'beginning' to time and space. Given the reference to the pea, the instanton became popularly known as the 'pea instanton'.

Like a good number of Hawking's theories, the pea instanton provoked all manner of controversies. Many physicists did not accept the notion of imaginary time, which played a starring role

Hawking married Elaine Mason in 1995, although the couple would divorce nine years later.

151

in the instanton theory, and disliked the use of quantum mechanics as a theory of universal inflation, the lack of a singularity and the unlikelihood of any experimental validation. The instanton showed that Hawking was never bound by the opinion of others, nor did he shy away from challenging his own ideas of the past. Hawking was prepared to go where the maths, logic and vision took him, although of course that did not mean he was always right.

PERSONAL EFFECTS

Even as Hawking was looking to the heavens, earth-bound experience was pressing in hard from the sides. Nowhere was this more apparent than in his marriage to Jane. As Hawking described the situation in his autobiography, he progressively became more unhappy with the relationship between her and Jonathan, to the stage that in 1990 he moved out of the family home to live in a flat in Cambridge with his nurse, Elaine Mason.[108] In Kitty Ferguson's extensive biography, however, the real reason the marriage broke down came when Hawking announced he and Elaine had begun a relationship.[109]

The end of the marriage is most fully recounted in Jane Hawking's own book about her life with Stephen. She details with deep emotional insight not only her loving, complicated, but ultimately exhausting relationship with Hawking, but also her brittle relationship with Elaine. The separation meant practical adjustments had to be made, including for Elaine, who at this time was married to David Mason and had two young children; she divorced him in 1994. Together, the new couple found their flat accommodation too small for their needs. As a solution, they purchased a plot of university land, on which they built a new home, one that was suited to Hawking's complex requirements. David and Elaine were married on 16 September 1995, while Jane and Jonathan married in July 1997.

The breakdown of any marriage is often tinged with sadness, but that of Jane and Stephen Hawking was particularly poignant. For all Hawking's formidable reserves of will and intellect, it seems hard to argue that much of the stability underpinning his success came from the love, belonging and support provided by Jane over his many years of progressive decline. When they divorced, they had been married nearly 25 years, and those had been astonishing years of transformation for Hawking, at every level of life. Jane provided much of the continuity, as well as giving Hawking a family he adored.

Jane would consequently have her own successful career as an educator and writer. Although she moved on, towards the end of the 1990s it was evidently time to put her own side of the story. Her 1999 book *Music to Move the Stars: A Life with Stephen* (updated and republished in 2013 as *Travelling to Infinity: The True Story Behind the Theory of Everything*) was an intimate and heartfelt account of her years with Hawking. Such was the power of the narrative that it inspired the 2004 biographical television film *Hawking*, written by British screenwriter Peter Moffat and directed by Philip Martin. The challenging titular role was played by Benedict Cumberbatch with such authenticity that he won the Golden Nymph (the prize awarded within the Official Competition of the Monte-Carlo Television Festival) for Best Performance by an Actor in a TV Film or Miniseries. He would not be the last actor to take on this most challenging of roles.

BRIGHTEST STAR

Hawking more than made his mark in the 1980s, but it was in the 1990s that he transitioned to global superstar. The initial drive behind that success was certainly the triumph of his first books. Those who invested the time to read *A Brief History of Time* or *The Universe in a Nutshell* felt both improved and enlightened, and he consequently built up a large and loyal readership. But even for those who never looked at a single page of Hawking's writing, he attained near-universal recognition and respect. How he managed to do so is a lesson in the exponential nature of public promotion.

Much of the credit for his stardom must surely go to the power of television. Millions of people worldwide knew already through print and news media that Hawking was a profoundly disabled, profoundly brilliant scientist, one whom everyone from Hollywood celebrities to heads of state appeared eager to meet. That package was perfectly suited to television exposure. Hawking had already featured in interviews and documentaries in the 1970s and 1980s, but in the 1990s his screen time was raised in both duration and impact.

A critical event came early in the decade, in 1991. In that year, a feature film version of Hawking's *A Brief History of Time* premiered in Los Angeles, New York and Colorado and was rolled out internationally in 1992. Hawking was clearly moving well beyond the realms of TV specials and interviews. The film was the brainchild of American educator and film producer Gordon Freedman who, inspired by Hawking's eponymous book, sold the idea to the Anglia Television company in the UK. The film would thereafter be a joint production between Anglia Television (with Anglia's David Hickman as producer), Freedman's production company Janus Films, and also Tokyo Broadcasting.

Freedman's vision for the film was not just to transfer the great ideas of *A Brief History of Time* into 80 minutes of big-screen viewing. He also wanted to capture some of the personality and life of Hawking himself, making the film a biographical as well as a conceptual work. The choice of director was critical, so Freedman consulted none other than Steven Spielberg about who to choose. Spielberg recommended Errol Morris, a talented, visionary film director who also happened to have studied the history of physics at Princeton and philosophy at Berkeley, so was able to grasp the science behind the story. He also had something of a maverick personality, so would be well suited to working with Hawking.

The film that emerged is a beautifully composed work. Hawking himself explains much of the science, his synthetic voice achieving a form of elegance against graphics and other visuals that manifest the ideas. The beautifully atmospheric musical score was composed by Philip Glass, a highly respected American composer and pianist. The film gave many intimate insights. It showed, for example, in close detail Hawking's use of the Equalizer software, slow and ponderous, but also with an atmosphere of deeply peaceful concentration. But arguably the true power of the film came from the extensive interviews with family, friends and fellow scientists, showing Hawking as a man in context, not an isolated genius. The first words of the film are spoken by Hawking, but the scene soon after cuts to his mother, Isobel, whose grace and intelligence are immediately apparent: 'Luck? Luck? Well, we have been very lucky – I mean my family and Stephen and everybody. You have your disasters, but the point is that we have survived. Everybody has disasters, and yet some people are never seen again.' Her opening words are a humble reflection on how finely balanced outcomes can be, not least for her son. (Isobel Hawking died in 2013 at the age of 98; Frank Hawking had died well before her in 1986, at the age of 80.)

Hawking initially objected to the biographical focus within the film, but Morris, Spielberg and others would bring him round to the idea. Morris would later confess that he found his first meeting with Hawking intimidating: 'It was frightening ... Here's somebody who's completely physically incapacitated, someone who can't move, confined to a chair, can't speak, and yet, he's one of the most frightening people I've ever met. Call it ironic, whatever.'[110] In the same interview, Morris admitted that Jane Hawking would not contribute to the film, and that 'There was such anger about his relationship with the nurse, with Elaine Mason, that it was hard getting a lot of people to participate in the film.'[111] As was often the way with Hawking, however, the professional relationship between him and Morris turned into a long-lasting friendship.

The film went on to critical success and received several awards, including the 1992 Grand Jury Prize for Documentary Filmmaking and the Documentary Filmmaker's Trophy at the Sundance Festival and the Filmmaker's Award from the National Society of Film Critics. The film was also accompanied by a book, *A Brief History of Time: A Reader's Companion*, which provided a transcript of all the words spoken in the film, along with personal photographs.

POP CULTURE

As the 1990s progressed, Stephen Hawking proved he was willing

WORMS, STRINGS AND PEAS

to embrace pop-culture projects, for no other reason than they were simple fun. They also expanded his profile among an even wider audience.

Since childhood, Hawking had always been an enthusiastic fan of the *Star Trek* series and films. So it was a case of dreams come true when, in 1993, Hawking secured a brief cameo role in the TV series *Star Trek: The Next Generation*. The offer came after Hawking met the actor Leonard Nimoy, famed for playing Spock in the original series, at a party. Hawking confessed his fandom and Nimoy set the wheels in motion for an appearance. Hawking thus starred, albeit briefly, in Episode 26 ('Descent, Part 1'), Season 6. He played a holographic version of himself, sitting alongside holograms of Albert Einstein and Sir Isaac Newton and engaged in a game of poker with the physicists and the android Data.

Appearing in *Star Trek* sent the signal that Hawking was open

For Star Trek: The Next Generation, *Stephen Hawking played himself alongside Jim Norton as Albert Einstein and John Neville as Sir Isaac Newton.*

to more than just conference appearances and profile interviews. In 1999, Hawking appeared as a cartoon manifestation of himself in that cornerstone of modern American TV culture, *The Simpsons*, of which he was also a devoted fan. In Episode 22 ('They Saved Lisa's Brain'), Season 10, Hawking's character provides salvation and wisdom to a beleaguered Lisa, who is making a desperate effort to save Springfield from its own stupidity. (The parallels with how Hawking saw himself are there to be made.) At one point, he airlifts Lisa to safety from an angry mob by converting, at the push of a button, his wheelchair into a jet-assisted helicopter. (The mechanical transformation initially malfunctions, resulting in Hawking engaging the automatic teeth-brushing programme.) Hawking also finds himself sitting in Moe's Tavern, chatting to the illustrious Homer, and says: 'Your theory of a doughnut-shaped universe is intriguing Homer, I may have to steal it.' On which Homer reflects, 'Wow, I can't believe that someone I've never heard of is hanging out with me.' Hawking was never shy about self-mockery. He became a popular albeit occasional figure in *The Simpsons*; between 1999 and 2017 he appeared in six episodes, with either a significant role or a cameo appearance, all recorded with his own voice. (Hawking later wryly observed in an interview with Brian Cox that some members of the public thought Stephen Hawking was *only* a fictional *Simpsons* character.)

Between the media appearances, between the films and the books, between his research and his academic articles, Hawking travelled the world, making personal appearances and contributions at numerous events, often receiving awards in the process. During this time, we see more of Hawking's activist nature on

WORMS, STRINGS AND PEAS

display, particularly in relation to disabled rights.

Going back to 1990, in that year Hawking attended an occupational science conference held at the University of Southern California. In his speech at that event, Hawking made some impassioned observations about the way society treats the disabled, and the way that they regard themselves. First, he pushed back at the media effort to ennoble his own struggle: 'I find it a bit embarrassing, in that people think I have great courage. But it's not as if I had a choice and deliberately chose a difficult path. I have just done the only thing open to me in the situation.' He also vented his frustration at those who saw his motor neurone disease before they saw anything else: 'I would like to be thought of as a scientist who just happens to be disabled, rather than as a disabled scientist.' But there was no self-pity here. Instead, he wanted practical and cultural changes to integrate disabled young people more fully, rather than having them stuck on the sidelines in a form of 'apartheid', as he described it. His message to them was rousing: 'In my opinion, disabled people should concentrate on what they can do well, and should not try to compete in areas in which they will necessarily do less well than able-bodied people. They should aim to be the best period, not the best among the disabled.'[112] Hawking recognized that his increasingly visible status and, indeed, celebrity could be used for the public good, a platform from which he could champion important social and scientific messages and, occasionally, through which he could channel his anger.

The 1990s was thus yet another great decade for Hawking, albeit one of significant personal upheaval for him and his family, much to the interest of the same media who courted him. The scale of his achievements in the 1990s can be framed between

WORMS, STRINGS AND PEAS

Showing a customary disregard for physical limits, Hawking visit-ed the Antarctic in 1997.

two events at opposite ends of the decade. In 1990, Hawking received an honorary Doctorate of Science from Harvard University, taking the award at the Commencement ceremony. Another world-beating institution, this one in his beloved America, had recognized his greatness and contribution. If we now jump ahead to 1998, we see how Hawking's distinctive voice had attained global reach. On 6 March, in the East Room of the White House and at the personal invitation of President Bill Clinton, Hawking gave the second of the White House Millennium Lecture Series talks, a series that brought together some of the world's leading scholars, scientists and creators. The event was aired on C-SPAN and broadcast around the world by the BBC, as well as being aired on the internet via cybercast. Hawking's lecture was entitled 'Imagination and Change: Science in the Next Millennium'. The lecture began light-heartedly, with a reference to his appearance on *Star Trek* but it quickly morphed into something serious and substantial, a discussion about the threats to humanity and what scientists and society could do about it. As we shall see in the next chapter, Hawking's mature voice had much to say beyond physics.

CHAPTER 7
TO THE STARS

On 1 January 2000, Stephen Hawking entered a new millennium. For a man who should, by medical prediction, have been dead during the 1960s, he had shown an enormous defiance of fate. Taken in the round, Hawking was proving to be formidably robust.

In the 2000s, Hawking's intellectual effort continued to be channelled into theoretical physics and cosmology. It was also a time, however, in which he found another voice, one roused to address perceived social injustices, existential threats and political calamities. Hawking's views on these matters, as we shall see, did not command automatic respect or acceptance from the wider world. But Hawking knew, had always known, that ultimately his time on this Earth was limited. It was important for him to raise awareness of what he saw as the dangers, and the solutions, of the future.

MEDIA SPOTLIGHT

By the time the New Year clocks registered the year 2000, Hawking was in his late 50s. More than half of that life had been spent fighting an illness that took away most of his physical functionality. Undaunted, he went into the new millennium without taking his foot off the accelerator. He appeared to retain enormous energy, reflected in his endlessly demanding programme of commitments. In one year alone (2005), for example, he made seven international work trips, no mean feat when considering the attendant logistical challenges. And this was just a typical year.

Media interest in Hawking had been strong for decades now, but it had by no means peaked. In fact, in the 2000s it appeared to rise to something of a frenzy. Hawking appeared on many high-profile talk shows, including *Late Night with Conan O'Brien* and *Last Week Tonight with John Oliver*. In these, and other contexts, Hawking showed his stellar sense of humour. In 2016, Hawking reconnected with the *Star Trek* universe when he appeared in the documentary *The Truth is in the Stars*, hosted by none other than William Shatner (the actor famed for playing Captain James T. Kirk of the USS *Enterprise*). Also in the 'dream come true' category was when Hawking made a cameo appearance in a new radio adaptation of Douglas Adams' *The Hitchhiker's Guide to the Galaxy*. Hawking's voice features in the first episode, playing the role of 'Guide Mk II', a super-intelligent but villainous being.

The rise of the internet enabled Hawking's celebrity to spread to all corners of the globe. In April 2016, he expanded his already sizeable following by joining the Chinese social media platform Weibo, posting regularly on a variety of science and social topics. China was evidently hungry for Hawking – his site gained 140,000 Chinese followers in the first half an hour and 1.5 million in the first day. By 2018, that number was up to 4.6 million. Hawking also diversified. In 2017, he starred in a TV commercial for the UK insurance comparison site Go Compare, in which the brand's annoying opera singer was sucked into a black hole.

TV remained a medium through which Hawking gave further lessons in popular science, broadening his audience beyond those who consumed his books. In 2010, the mini-series *Stephen Hawking's Universe* (not to be confused with the 1997 PBS series of the same name, and in the USA named *Into the Universe with*

Stephen Hawking) was broadcast on the Discovery Channel. Each episode was written by Hawking, the narrative a mix of his voice and a voice-over by Benedict Cumberbatch. The episode list clearly tapped into the public appetite for some of the more sensational aspects of physics and cosmology (Episode 1: 'Aliens'; Episode 2: 'Time Travel'; Episode 3: 'The Story of Everything'), but Hawking understood that holding initial interest was critical to transferring deeper learning. The following year saw the release of another Hawking mini-series, *Brave New World with Stephen Hawking*. This series again hit keynotes among Hawking's wider interests, the respective topics of episodes 1–5 being Machines, Health, Technology, Environment and Biology.

Another Hawking TV moment to mention is *Stephen Hawking's Favorite Places*, a three-part mini-series broadcast in 2010. The imaginative conceit of the series was Hawking piloting the CGI-generated spaceship SS *Hawking*, using the vessel to visit places of professional and cosmological interest, from Santa Barbara in California to the star Proxima Centauri. In the same year, Hawking joined Professor Danielle George and Christophe Galfard on the BBC production *The Search for a New Earth*, in which the presenters explored the possibilities for human migration to other planets.

It could be tempting to see Hawking's TV work as a lucrative digression from the serious business of science. The money that came from such work, however, was not inconsequential to Hawking's life. Given the very high costs of his care, a constant and strong inflow of money was the foundation of many of the opportunities Hawking seized in life. Furthermore, Hawking never looked down upon popular science. Ultimately, science was there to be shared.

Lucy and Stephen Hawking discuss space education at NASA's 50th Anniversary celebrations in Washington DC, 21 April 2008.

What was certainly true, however, was that the new millennium saw Hawking given that most rare treatment for a scientist – a full-length Hollywood biopic for the big screen. The film was *The Theory of Everything* (2014). To recap, it was a film adaptation of Jane Hawking's 1999 memoir, *Travelling to Infinity: My Life with Stephen*. It was, therefore, primarily a love story, played out against the background of Hawking's academic ascent and physical descent, from the two protagonists meeting at Cambridge through to their marriage. The screenplay was the creation of New Zealand writer and filmmaker Anthony McCarten, who was assisted, after persuasion and reassurance, by Jane Hawking herself. The impressive young actor Eddie Redmayne played Hawking, matched by the equally capable Felicity Jones playing Jane. Both actors would be lauded for the authenticity of their performances, capturing the essence and mannerisms of their subjects.

The film was released from September 2014, to critical and commercial success. A feature movie about a profoundly disabled theoretical physicist might not sound like the most commercial pitch, but it brought in box-office revenues of $123 million, far exceeding the $15 million production budget. The film and its stars garnered numerous awards, including five Academy Award nominations, ten British Academy Film Awards (BAFTA) nominations and four Golden Globe Award nominations, winning in many of the categories. Eddie Redmayne won an Oscar, a BAFTA and a Golden Globe for his acting. Hawking's personal life, as well as his science, was now immortalized.

HARD LANDINGS

Hawking's personal life was rarely as straightforward as his professional life. In 2006, Hawking and Elaine filed for divorce, the separation completed the following year. In his autobiography, Hawking is tight-lipped about very personal family matters; he was always protective of his privacy. He simply stated that his various health crises 'took their emotional toll on Elaine'.[113] The press, however, had run deep with speculation and investigation during the years of their marriage. Certainly, there appears to have been a long period of troubles, and of conflict between Elaine and the wider Hawking family, especially with Lucy. In April 2005, the *Standard* published a lengthy interview with Lucy Hawking (to mark the publication of her first novel, *Jaded*), conducted by the journalist Emine Saner. Lucy guardedly expressed concerns when she thought back to the time of her father's marriage to Elaine and the impact it had on Hawking's relationship with his children: '"The fame and money arrive and – bingo! – dad's gone," says Lucy. "It's very difficult to talk about because being bitter is so unpleasant and not helpful but I think it's undeniable that there was an element of that at the time."' Saner confirmed that Lucy did not attend her father's wedding to Elaine. When asked about her own relationship with Elaine, Lucy refused to comment in-depth, and simple stated, 'I would be really happy for my father if I thought he was happy.'[114]

Saner then probed into another acutely personal subject for Lucy. By the beginning of the 2000s, occasional press rumours alleged Elaine was being controlling and manipulative towards her husband, and even that she had been physically abusive. According to a *Vanity Fair* article from 2004, when Hawking suffered a fractured wrist in 1999, he failed to provide an adequate explanation.[115] The concerns culminated in 2003 in an investigation by Cambridgeshire Police, after further accusations of physical

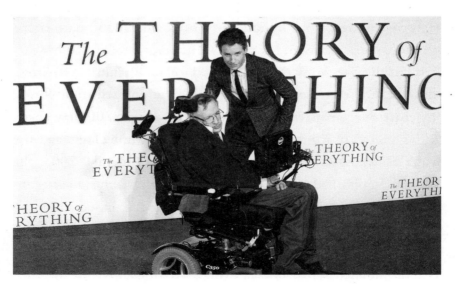

Stephen Hawking and actor Eddie Redmayne attend the UK premiere of The Theory of Everything, *9 December 2014.*

mistreatment. Some of the reported charges made for serious reading, including leaving Hawking without access to a urine bottle so he wet himself, gashing his cheek with a razor, breaking his wrist by banging his arm into his wheelchair and leaving him unattended in a hot garden so that he suffered sunburn and dehydration.[116] Hawking himself resisted the investigation, and the charges were subsequently dropped. In her interview with Saner, Lucy Hawking expressed that his physical well-being 'continues to be a subject of great concern', but that she appreciated her father was a very private man and also someone who would baulk at the idea he wasn't in control.

Hawking's own short account of his life with Elaine, in *My Brief History*, acknowledges that as a couple he and Elaine were volatile, 'passionate and tempestuous'.[117] He also gave due credit to Elaine as his carer, however, someone who quite literally saved Hawking's life on several occasions. That observation was obviously, for Hawking, an important counterbalance to press coverage of the failed marriage.

By the time of his divorce, certainly, Hawking had experienced many further brushes with death. He was hospitalized with serious pneumonia in December 2003, and in November 2005, while in the USA, he had to be resuscitated after his breathing failed. Those around Hawking also began to notice a subtle but real weakening, a decline in his energy levels, as he progressed from his 60th to his 70th birthday.

His changing condition brought challenges for his communications technology. By 2006, Hawking was operating the selector switch for his voice computer through an interface that pressed against his cheek muscle; he essentially made a squinting action with one eye to select lines or words on the screen. As he became frailer, even that became harder to use. From 2007, he was fortunate to be accompanied by a highly capable new technical assistant, engineering graduate Sam Blackburn. He made important improvements to the existing technology, including fitting an enhanced 'blink switch' for Hawking's computer interactions. But it was clear that Hawking's future would require more technological support.

Fortune again smiled on Hawking. In 1997, Hawking had met the co-founder of the Intel computer company, Gordon Moore, at a conference. Moore had the chance to watch Hawking's computer working in real time, and offered to upgrade the computer hardware and provide technical support free of charge on a rolling basis every 18 months. By 2011, even the blink switch was more of a struggle, particularly as Hawking tired in the later parts of the day, and the interface became clunkier to use. Intel again stepped up and formed a dedicated five-person team to improve the software interface. The team included project head Lama Nachman, who was the director of the Anticipatory Computing Lab; Horst Haussecker, the director of the Experience Technology Lab; and Pete Denman, an interaction designer, who as a paraplegic also knew the challenges of using technology.

Between 2012 and 2018, the Intel team were in frequent huddles over improvements and innovations to Hawking's communications suite. This was no easy matter. Over many years, Hawking had developed a working process that, for all its imperfections, suited him, based upon now-aging technology. While eye-tracking selection systems, advanced word-prediction software and other solutions were offered, and some partially adopted, Hawking could be resistant to change. But over time, the Intel team gave Hawking's computer interactions more speed and flexibility, especially through an interface called the 'Assistive Context-Aware Toolkit' (ACAT), which used more logically arranged contextual menus to improve functions such as app switching, internet searching and email. Denman also changed the optical boundaries of Hawking's observed universe by simply fitting a mirror to the edge of the computer screen, meaning that Hawking could see people and objects to his sides or rear without having to strain his eyes. With such support, Hawking was able to maintain his active life despite the further impediments of age and disability.

THE FINAL THEORY?

Was Hawking still relevant? As he advanced into the new millennium, some scientists felt that his physics was old school, no longer at the cutting edge of research and ideas. Any such conclusions were proved premature. What is extraordinary about the last 18 years of Hawking's life is how vigorously he threw himself into the great debates of contemporary physics, right to the very end. At the same time, he continued his mission to spread science to the masses.

A starting point for Hawking's 21st-century research is his collaboration with the Belgian cosmologist Thomas Hertog in the mid-2000s, developing the models of the no-boundary multiverse. This work was laid down in the 2006 paper 'Populating the Landscape: A Top Down Approach'. In the paper, Hawking and Hertog presented a topographical landscape consisting of multiple universes arising from an initial quantum state. The beginning of our universe, indeed of all universes, contained within it all possible future outcomes, much like the particle wave function in quantum mechanics. To make sense of this from humanity's perspective, they advocated what they called a 'top-down approach', in which the observer starts with the universe as it stands in the present configuration, then from this position 'one computes amplitudes for alternative histories of the universe with final boundary conditions only'.[118] In effect, our observation of the universe collapses the wave function to give us our specific history of the universe, including its inflationary model. Hawking distinguished this theory from its alternative: 'In a cosmology based on eternal inflation there is only one universe with a fractal structure at late times, whereas in top down cosmology one envisions a set of alternative universes, which are more likely to be homogeneous, but with different values for various effective coupling constants.'[119] Not all of this is accessible to the general reader, but the importance of the observer in this model was a theme to which we shall return shortly.

In the new millennium Hawking also plunged back into the ever-lively information paradox debate. We might remember that Hawking's original position was that the information that went into a black hole could be lost irrevocably once the black hole evaporated due to the mass depletion from Hawking radiation. This, as many pointed out, was a radical violation of the laws of physics. Hawking's position began to shift over time, however, and especially by the early 2000s. At this time, the new leader in the information paradox debate was the Argentinian physicist Juan Martín Maldacena, who provided a breakthrough with his mathematical models, notably the 'AdS/CFT correspondence'. This work gave strong theoretical support for Susskind's theory of holographic information preservation, suggesting that information in a black hole could be encoded on its event horizon.

In response, Hawking was moved to revise his own position further, an action he explained at the 17th International Conference on General Relativity and Gravitation in Dublin in 2004. Never one for understatement, Hawking boldly began his presentation with the declaration: 'I want to report that I think I have solved a major problem in theoretical physics.' He now rejected the argument that black holes destroy the information that falls into them. Instead, that information can be stored in quantum fluctuations at the event horizon, although the information was in a scrambled and encoded form. In the process, Hawking openly conceded a bet he and Kip Thorne had made with Caltech's John Preskill back in 1997, over Preskill's contention that the information in a black hole could indeed be recovered. Hawking's revised theories of black holes also fed into work with physicists Malcolm Perry and Andrew Strominger, who in the 2010s together offered the theory that black holes had 'soft hair', consisting of certain low-energy particles on the event horizon that could store the information of the particles that went into the void.

Hawking's final academic paper, the terminus of an intellectual chain stretching back to the 1960s, came in April 2018. 'A Smooth Exit from Eternal Inflation?' was another Hawking–Hertog collaboration, the title of the paper suggesting both possibility and an uncertainty.[120] In the paper, they questioned the model of inflation as advanced by Andrei Linde. That model, specifically, was that the universe was in a process of eternal inflation, with individual universes (plural – this was a multiverse model) appearing as pockets in the expansion. Linde's gustatory analogy was to imagine an infinitely expanding block of Swiss cheese; the trademark holes in the cheese are the universes.

Hawking and Hertog attempted to put some limits on this model to avoid the problematic mathematical infinities it produced. Using a revised version of the no-boundary proposal, and applying string theory and quantum gravity, they argued that the actual number of universes could be not only *finite*, but in some cases so similar to our own that we could make observational predictions about them. From that basis, a testable framework of the multiverse theory became more possible.

There was, of course, a question mark at the end of the title – Hawking and Hertog were not offering a slam-dunk theory. It has often been said that Hawking's gift to physics was his ability to find a new set of questions to answer, not necessarily the answers themselves. This does not mean, however, that Hawking was averse to making grand claims.

GOD AND MODEL-DEPENDENT REALISM

In 2010, the world's bookshelves were treated to another of Hawking's public-facing science books. This was *The Grand Design: New Answers to the Ultimate Questions of Life*, co-authored with Leonard Mlodinow. Unlike some of Hawking's earlier books, and particularly *A Brief History of Time*, opinion on *The Grand Design* was far more colourful, with a significant number of negative press reviews. Some critics felt that it said little different from previous publications and simply represented a new income stream for the Hawking industry. Others argued that Hawking used the book to raise questions, but moved on too quickly from actually giving us answers. Some took exception to what they saw as ill-founded attacks on theology and academic philosophy (to which we shall turn shortly).

Seen in the context of Hawking's long-running work in *popular* science, however, I would argue that *The Grand Design* is one of his most engaging works. It provides an accessible (mostly) introduction to the history of physics, fundamental theories and positions of cosmology, theoretical physics and quantum mechanics, without the cognitive overload of some of his previous books. The book also extends previous work in some genuinely fresh directions, including the top-down cosmology and the multiverse theories we have already discussed.

The book is also one of Hawking's final statements on a Theory of Everything. In his view, the best chance for the unified explanation of the universe lies in M-theory (see the previous chapter). He puts his case straightforwardly: 'We now have a candidate for the ultimate theory of everything, if indeed one exists, called M-theory.'[121] He uses a cartographic analogy to make the case. Most maps of the world today are made using the Mercator projection, in which the spherical globe is essentially opened out to form a flat two-dimensional map with longitude and latitude lines imposed over it in a right-angled grid. The inherent problem with the Mercator projection is that it distorts the relative size of some countries the further you go north or south, making them appear far bigger than they are in reality. (Greenland, for example, is wildly exaggerated.) A more accurate map, therefore, would consist of individual maps each accurately covering a more limited area of the Earth's surface, the maps then formed into a composite with overlapping edges. Collectively, these maps present a more faithful view of the world. M-theory is much like this improved map, in that each theory has limited range, but collectively they form a comprehensive model.

One of the new arguments in *The Grand Design* is 'model-dependent realism'. The basic premise here is that there is no single reality 'out there' in the universe, but rather reality is dependent upon the individual's model of that reality. As human beings, we take in sensory data and apply an interpretation to it, one that works with our observations. Thus, Hawking points out, a goldfish in a circular bowl would be able to form a perfectly consistent theory of the laws of nature outside the bowl, despite the fact (or rather *because* of the fact) that the world beyond appears curved on account of the optical distortion of the bowl. At times, the argument almost has a postmodern flavour:

> When such a model is successful at explaining events, we tend to attribute to it, and to the elements and concepts that constitute it, the quality of reality or absolute truth. But there may be different ways in which one could model the same physical situation, with each employing different fundamental elements and concepts. If two such physical theories or models accurately predict the same events, one cannot be said to be more real than the other; rather, we are free to use whichever model is most convenient.[122]

Model-dependent realism makes the important point that there is no theory, no reality, *independent of us*. And theories such as quantum mechanics, alternative histories and holographic theory can lend weight to this position scientifically. We might here feel that Hawking is about to collapse into pure relativism, but arguably – there is some room for interpretation – he pulls back from that abyss. One key point he makes is that when it comes to models of reality, there are models and there are *good* models. The good model…

1. Is elegant
2. Contains few arbitrary or adjustable elements
3. Agrees with and explains all existing observations
4. Makes detailed predictions about future observations that can disprove or falsify the model if they are not borne out.[123]

The good model is important to arbitrate when alternative theories overlap or compete with one another directly. Even though in principle both are valid for the user, *testing* the model could significantly change the individual's relationship with reality.

Admittedly, *The Grand Design* remains a little frustrating on model-dependent realism, as it falls slightly short in explanations about validating models in conflict with other models, and what that process itself says about reality. And this gets to the heart of one of the key criticisms about the book. In the introduction, Hawking and Mlodinow make a list of some of the great questions we ask of life, the universe and reality. They then proceed to make a particularly bold claim: 'Traditionally these are questions for philosophy, but philosophy is dead. Philosophy has not kept up with modern developments in science, particularly physics. Scientists have become the bearers of the torch of discovery in our quest for knowledge.'[124]

Understandably, this statement aroused the ire of academic philosophers. One line of response was that Hawking was making pronouncements on domains he didn't really understand in depth. Philosophers and cultural commentators were quick to point out that philosophy had evolved as much as science in the 1990s and 2000s, and indeed that there were new branches of philosophy that were a response to the scientific and technological age, especially in relation to ethics and reality. Furthermore, concepts such as model-dependent realism and the anthropic principle were ripe with potential for philosophical analysis.

Another key area of controversy was Hawking's pronouncements on God. In the past, Hawking had made statements that those of faith could extract and use to back their theological position. At a Vatican conference in 2008, for example, he stated: 'I believe the universe is governed by the laws of science. The laws may have been decreed by God, but God does not intervene to break the laws.' But throughout his career, Hawking had never lent his authority to the idea of a personal creator God, and in *The Grand Design* he was more emphatic about his lack of need for divine explanations.

As in *A Brief History of Time*, *The Grand Design* God does have a starring role in the discussion, but without any authority. One of the first references to God in the book states explicitly that the universe doesn't require a creator God to exist, just physical laws.[125] Hawking and Mlodinow trace a basic history of religious faith, and how natural disasters, heavenly bodies and the cycles of nature were ascribed to divine origins, for want of more informed explanations. The authors make an argument for theological redundancy: we have arrived at the point where science can answer three big questions – Why is there something rather than nothing? Why do we exist? Why this particular set of laws and not some other? – without any recourse to a divine agent.

Hawking's position on God in *The Grand Design* was echoed elsewhere in the 2000s. In *Brief Answers to the Big Questions* he had addressed the question 'Do I have faith?' head-on: 'We are free to believe what we want, and it's my view that the simplest explanation is that there is no God.'[126] In an interview with the *Guardian*, he was harsher when discussing any notions of immortality: 'I regard the brain as a computer which will stop working when its components fail. There is no heaven or afterlife for broken down computers; that is a fairy story for people afraid of the dark.'[127] Hawking was certainly an atheist (as he stated directly in an interview for the Spanish newspaper *El Mundo*), but he perhaps saw a surrogate religion, embodied in the rites and rituals of physics: 'God is the name people give to the reason we are here. But I think that reason is the laws of physics rather than someone with whom one can have a personal relationship. An impersonal God.'[128] This statement, given to *Time* magazine, shows that for Hawking physics was not just a dry intellectual pursuit, it was rather a beautiful act of scientific wonder.

CAMPAIGNER FOR THE FUTURE

Hawking never lived in a purely academic bubble. He understood that many of the world's people faced problems more existentially pressing than the information paradox. Thus from the moment he attended his first 'ban the bomb' marches in the 1960s, political activism was a counterpoint to his scientific endeavours. In the last two decades of Hawking's life, however, his rising fame gave him a far more influential platform from which to speak out.

Politically, Hawking was to the left of the spectrum, but the issues he addressed from this position were principled and contentious. In 2004, for example, he spoke out vigorously against the US-led invasion of Iraq at an anti-war rally held in London's Trafalgar Square, telling the crowd in unequivocal terms that the conflict was based on the lies of the Western governments and that coalition troops should be withdrawn immediately. In 2013, after some lobbying by other academics (including Noam Chomsky), Hawking was persuaded to boycott his attendance at the annual Israeli Presidential Conference, in protest over what he saw as Israel's unjust treatment of the Palestinians. His action against the conference, which brought together world leaders and thinkers of all disciplines, attracted high-profile criticism. David Newman, then dean of the faculty of Humanities and Social Sciences at Ben-Gurion University, said that the boycott 'just destroys one of the very few spaces left where Israelis and Palestinians actually do come together'.

The politically turbulent 2000s gave Hawking many other opportunities to engage with issues of the day. He decried the outcome of the Brexit vote in 2016, with particular concern over its impact on European-wide scientific collaboration. Looking incredulously across the Atlantic, he was also similarly despairing over the election of Donald Trump to President of the United States. Prior to the voting day, Hawking was asked to explain Trump's apparent popularity: '"I can't," Hawking replied. "He is a demagogue who seems to appeal to the lowest common denominator."'[129]

Hawking was also, understandably, a strong advocate for public health care. He put his head above the parapet on more than one occasion to take issue with political decisions related to the NHS, an institution without which, he declared, he would not be alive. In August 2017, he entered into a much-publicized spat with UK Conservative politician Jeremy Hunt, who up until recently had been the government's Health Secretary. Hawking accused Hunt of implementing policies that had crippled the NHS and of abusing scientific data to back his arguments, an act that in turn

Hawking felt undermined public trust in science. Hunt and Hawking went at each other verbally in the press. Hawking was also part of a group of academics who launched a subsequent legal action against the formation of Accountable Care Organizations (ACOs) – a form of medical care provision used in the USA – within NHS England. They were successful in imposing a consultative delay in the legislative process.

Hawking retained something approaching hero status to many in the disabled community. There was no more fitting testimony to his empowering voice than when, on 29 August 2012, Hawking took centre stage in the dazzling opening ceremony to the Paralympics in London. His stadium address included passages of simple, inclusive power:

> The Paralympic Games is also about transforming the perceptions of the World. We are all different. There is no such thing as a standard or run of the mill human being – but we share the same human spirit. What is important is that we have the ability to create. This creativity can take many forms – from physical achievements to theoretical physics. However difficult life may seem, there is always something you can do, and succeed at.[130]

These words remind us that Hawking was a fine and versatile writer, with wide range in style and content, capable of reaching out to the 'human spirit' as much as the intellect.

As Hawking moved through his 60s and into his 70s, he seemed to recognize that it was important to look to a future that lay beyond his own time on Earth. In the years leading up to his death, he threw increasing effort into highlighting what he saw as the imminent dan-

President Barack Obama talks with Hawking before presenting him with the Presidential Medal of Freedom, the highest civilian honour in the United States, at the White House on 12 August 2009.

gers faced by the human race. He also provided solutions of wildly diverse ambition. Many of his arguments were captured in *Brief Answers to the Big Questions*, a single-volume collection of important speeches and articles, published just after his death.

Hawking spent his professional life looking to the stars. This cosmological gaze turned into something approaching an end-of-days action plan, specifically that we humans should look to the heavens as our future, rather than the limitations of Earth. This view is defined in two of Hawking's related essays: 'Will we survive on Earth?' and 'Should we colonize space?'

Hawking's answer to the first question could be summarized as 'Maybe, but the odds don't look good.' In the essay, Hawking accepts that the 'universe is a violent place', with random natural phenomena such as supernovae and asteroids lurking out there, waiting to erase life as we know it, in the same way an asteroid wiped out the dinosaurs 66 million years ago. To cheer the reader, he reassures us that the repeat of such a cataclysmic strike is not an improbability, but rather one that 'is guaranteed by the laws of physics and probability'.

But the core concern of 'Will we survive on Earth?' is not random celestial events, but rather the nature and behaviour of humanity itself. Hawking fears that human beings will ultimately be the source of their own destruction. This is one area of his psyche where he seemed to approach gloomy fatalism: 'The Earth is under threat from so many areas that it is difficult for me to be positive. The threats are too big and too numerous.'

Hawking highlighted three concerns in particular. First was population growth, an issue made existential by humanity's careless attitude to natural resources, with insatiable consumption and cavalier destruction. The results were widespread – extinct animal species, deforestation, water scarcity, disease, war, crop failures. For Hawking, there was a blind clumsiness and cruelty in human society at large that he appears to have found profoundly depressing – 'We can be an ignorant, unthinking lot', he sighed in the essay.

The second of the great challenges for human survival was global warming. The true danger of climate change is its time-sensitive nature, Hawking declared impatiently – the world needed to act, and *now*, if it is to prevent global warming becoming self-sustaining through effects such as melted ice caps (the smaller the ice caps, the less solar energy is reflected back into space) and rainforest deforestation (rainforests are some of the largest natural sinks of global carbon dioxide). This problem was made worse, he argued, by the proliferation of climate-change deniers, who he felt bled the urgency from the need to act. His nightmare vision was of Earth eventually having a climate like that of Venus, heat-blasted by the Sun to 250 °C (482 °F), with clouds raining sulphuric acid.

His final major worry about humanity was the possibility of nuclear war. Hawking's resistance to global arsenals of nuclear weapons stretched back to his teenage years. He begins 'Will we survive on Earth?' with an update (in 2018) on the status of the Doomsday Clock, the metaphorical timepiece created by former research scientists from the Manhattan Project in 1947, used to visualize how close the world was to civilization-ending nuclear war. If the clock struck 12 midnight, it was all over. In January 2018, Hawking observed, it was at two minutes to midnight. He acknowledged that nuclear arsenals were much reduced from the high-noon stand-off of the Cold War, but pointed out that there were still enough nuclear weapons to wipe out the world several times over, plus plenty of rogue states, crazed leaders and apocalyptic terrorist groups who might initiate a nuclear conflict.

Hawking's feelings about nuclear weapons play around a tension in his thinking about science. Hawking was at his most optimistic when reflecting upon the solutions that science could bring to the world's great problems. In the essay, he speaks about the fact that human beings are at their best when they are united in exploratory curiosity, demonstrated by globally unifying, technologically progressive events such as the 1969 Apollo 11 Moon landing. But for all his belief in the scientific method and advanced technologies, Hawking was not a utopian when it came to scientific progress. He saw clearly that the present world was in a phase of tremendous scientific acceleration, particularly in the emerging technology of Artificial Intelligence (AI).

As someone whose life had been facilitated by advanced computer technology, we might expect Hawking to have been a passionate advocate for AI. He certainly saw AI as rich in potential, not least for progressing science beyond the limitations of human intelligence, at least in terms of data processing. He also argued, in his essay 'Will artificial intelligence outsmart us?', that in the medium term at least AI could automate many people's jobs, resulting in 'both great prosperity and equality' (although the exact mechanism of these outcomes is rather underexplained).[131] AI held out promise, but Hawking was also deeply concerned about the weights on the opposite side of the balance scales. As a long-standing campaigner against nuclear weapons, for example, Hawking accepted AI could, probably would, be repurposed for new generations of autonomous weapons. AI might also reach levels of independence and power at which it could manipulate politics and financial markets to its own ends, or even that AI would start to regard human beings as an inconvenience to its own goals, and wipe them out.

On the matter of AI, therefore, Hawking was prepared to go beyond anxious nail-biting. He openly pushed for research and regulation to control some of AI's most threatening possibilities. In January 2015, he put his name to an open letter from the Future of Life Institute, a letter that to date has attracted more than 11,000 prominent signatories. The letter recognized AI's scope to yield significant achievements and insights for humanity, but also that humanity needed a better grasp on all its possible histories:

> There is now a broad consensus that AI research is progressing steadily, and that its impact on society is likely to increase. The potential benefits are huge, since everything that civilization has

to offer is a product of human intelligence; we cannot predict what we might achieve when this intelligence is magnified by the tools AI may provide, but the eradication of disease and poverty are not unfathomable. Because of the great potential of AI, it is important to research how to reap its benefits while avoiding potential pitfalls.[132]

In October of the following year, Hawking spoke at the launch of the Leverhulme Centre for the Future of Intelligence (CFI) in Cambridge, an organization that co-ordinated the work of four world-beating universities (Cambridge, Oxford, Berkeley and Imperial College, London) to explore the future possible impacts of AI on human society. In his address, Hawking accepted that AI could take humanity in one of two directions: 'The rise of powerful AI will either be the best or the worst thing ever to happen to humanity. We do not yet know which.'[133]

The case of AI is a good example of how Hawking understood that permanent exponential growth in human progress was not a necessary or permanent state of affairs. Like a giant star collapsing under its own gravity, progress could have its logical limits. He points out, for example, that if electricity consumption continued at its present rate, by the year 2600 it would 'make the world glow red hot'.[134] Furthermore, if the output of scientific papers maintained its exponential growth trajectory, then by the same year there would be ten papers in theoretical physics published every second. Hawking saw that we are in a problematic growth phase, but one that will not last forever.

In the present and immediate future, therefore, how could we address the global threats he raises? One option Hawking explored was the possibility that genetic engineering could enable human beings to exit the long grind of natural evolution and enter the new era of 'self-designed evolution'. Not only could genetic engineering modify DNA to eradicate diseases such as cystic fibrosis and muscular dystrophy, but in time, conceivably, it could be used to enhance human intelligence or to prune out undesirable qualities such as aggression. It might even 'be possible to use genetic engineering to make DNA-based life survive indefinitely, or at least for 100,000 years'.[135] Hawking also well understood the dangers inherent in the possibility of genetic-level human engineering; he recognized the nightmare scenario in which a new race of upgraded 'superhumans' – those who have all the power and influence – emerge, disease-resistant and intellectually brilliant, while the 'unimproved' humans are left to die out, or at least become 'unimportant'.[136]

Hawking's moral position on such outcomes is actually surprisingly hard to tease out. While there is much that is terrifying about the superhuman scenario, he seemed to accept that humanity would not be capable of resisting the temptations and possibilities of genetic engineering, even in the face of global laws that attempt to restrict it. Science will lead where it will, although humanity should do its level best to make sure that direction is positive.

And that led Hawking to look upwards to space. While in no way diminishing the challenges that lay ahead, Hawking was a firm advocate for future space colonization. In his essay 'Should we colonize space?', Hawking refers to his comment after a 2007 zero-gravity flight (see the Conclusion), in which he said he feared humanity would not survive if it did not go into space. In his essay, he doubled down on that point, emphasizing that 'I believed it

TO THE STARS

then, and I believe it still.'[137] In a March 2014 keynote address in New York in front of the Explorers Club Annual Dinner, Hawking expressed his conviction that, 'Not to leave planet Earth would be like castaways on a desert island not trying to escape.'[138]

Also present at the event as a speaker was Elon Musk, known not only as the intermittent world's richest man, former owner of PayPal and creator of the Tesla electric vehicle company, but also as the head of the private space company SpaceX. By 2014, Musk's vision for a pioneering private space programme was already a reality, having successfully launched orbital rockets and made the first commercial cargo flight to the International Space Station (ISS). Hawking and Musk had a shared passion for space colonization, and for many other global issues. Hawking predicted that human beings could have a permanent base on the Moon within 30 years, reach Mars in the next 50 years, and begin exploring the outer planets in the next 200 years; obviously automated systems could perform these feats earlier, leading the way for the humans behind them. Musk's vision for the colonization of Mars is on roughly the same timeline, although evidently much remains to be done.

In terms of practical steps to realize the vision of space colonization, Hawking suggested a global increase in the space budget by 20 times, raising it to a quarter of a per cent of global GDP. Pushing back against those who would argue that such money is far better spent on Earthly challenges, he argued, 'Isn't our future worth a quarter of a per cent?'[139] And he also thought of practicalities. Noting emerging research that suggests human bodies are simply not suited to long-term exposure to zero-gravity conditions, Hawking countered (in many ways failing to address the key points) that any extra-planetary base could be dug into the surface of the planet to provide thermal insulation and protect the inhabitants from thermal rays.

Hawking decided to put more skin in the game of space exploration when in 2016 he became a founding member of the Breakthrough Starshot project, alongside the Soviet-born Israeli entrepreneur and physicist Yuri Milner and the social media pioneer Mark Zuckerberg. Breakthrough Starshot is an ambitious programme in interstellar exploration. The proof-of-concept goal is to send thousands of tiny, ultralight 'nanobots' across space at speeds of about one-fifth of the speed of light, driven by powerful laser beams fired out from Earth, these engaging with 'light sails' on the backs of the craft. The first objective is to conduct a fly-by mission of Alpha Centauri; it would take 20 years for the craft to reach the star. During a news conference at the founding, Hawking declared that, 'The limit that confronts us now is the great void between us and the stars, but now we can transcend it.' It was a first step in what Hawking saw as part of a new era of space exploration. The impulse to escape Earth-bound limitations was strong in Hawking, and vigorously argued.

In a similar context, it should be noted, Hawking held the view that there was scant possibility of contact by, or even the existence of, alien life forms. The probabilities of life evolving elsewhere in the universe, and certainly of that life evolving to advanced intelligence, were extremely remote. He also reflected on the likelihood that any civilization that reached higher intelligence before us might well have wiped itself out by now – the jury is out on whether intelligence is actually an advantage to long-term survival. Nevertheless, Hawking conceded that aliens might exist somewhere out there, but generally discouraged efforts to contact them, believing that contact between us and a superior species might not work out in our favour. It might be rather like the technologically advanced Spanish meeting the indigenous Americans in the 15th and 16th centuries, noting how badly that turned out for the native peoples.

THE END

Hawking's declining health has been a steady drumbeat throughout this book. His health had been deteriorating since the 1960s, a long period of attrition for any human being to endure. On the way, however, Hawking had survived not only the daily trials, but also many sudden and life-threatening emergencies. Hawking was tough, and people knew it, ascribing to him something of an invincible quality. But Hawking's sense of mortality was always sober. Time, he knew, was only borrowed, and hence when he was alive, he threw himself into every present moment.

In early March 2018, Hawking was again hospitalized, although following treatment he moved back home. Again, many outsiders expected the predictable pull-through. This time it did not come. Stephen Hawking died on 14 March 2018.

The news of his death sent front-page ripples around the world. Those who expressed their sadness at his death went well beyond family, friends and colleagues to include world leaders, esteemed scientists and celebrities, but also a general public who had learned so much from this one man. It was clear than an astonishing life had come to a close.

While alive, Hawking was a true internationalist, but his home was ultimately England. Nothing spoke finer words about his legacy than his final resting place. After a moving funeral service in Cambridge, attended by thousands of well-wishers, he was

TO THE STARS

Hawking's funeral cortege moves through the streets of Cambridge on 31 March 2018.

interred in Westminster Abbey, burial place of kings, queens and luminaries from across a thousand years of British history. Entirely appropriately, his grave is next to that of Isaac Newton.

CONCLUSION

On 26 April 2007, Stephen Hawking literally escaped the bounds of gravity, a force that had absorbed much of his professional thinking, for a total duration of four minutes. Alongside his nurse practitioner, Nicola O'Brien, Hawking was taken aboard a modified Boeing 727 aircraft owned by Zero-Gravity Corporation (Zero-G). The aircraft was designed to put itself into a series of parabolic arcs, momentarily creating conditions of weightlessness for those in its specially adapted cabin. (Aircraft of this type are used to train astronauts for the experience of zero gravity.) Aided by flight crew, Hawking was able to experience the partial release from his physical limitations. In his pre-flight press conference, he said: 'I have been wheelchair-bound for almost four decades and the chance to float free in zero g will be wonderful.' After his flight, he described the experience as 'true freedom ... I was Superman for those few minutes'.

It was entirely appropriate that this life-affirming moment provided one of the photographs displayed at his funeral on 31 March 2018. For Stephen Hawking was a self-declared optimist. Given that here was a person who had contended with a dreadful degenerative condition for all of his adult life, his optimism says much about his force of character, his determination to play the cards as they were dealt. As we have seen, Hawking was not naive, nor was he ignorant to the forces of entropy seemingly at work in human psychology, society and politics. So what were the grounds for his optimism?

CONCLUSION

Despite the depredations of motor neurone disease, Hawking had known the love and affection of others, had been married and produced a family he adored, had many friends within and outside academia, and had known astonishing professional and commercial success. His optimism, therefore, may well have been earned simply through a life well lived. But beyond his personal world, Hawking was optimistic about science, *because* of science.

Scientific curiosity was an irresistible source of energy for Stephen Hawking, burning like the nuclear reaction at the heart of a star. From the outset of his academic career, he resisted thinking small. His primary fields of study – cosmology and theoretical physics – often looked up and out, away from the confines of a physical frame, through the atmosphere above and into the vastness of space. Hawking was not content to tighten his focus on a narrow set of phenomena. Instead, he wanted to reach out to

A clearly exhilarated Stephen Hawking escapes the bounds of gravity, a force that played such a critical part in his intellectual journey.

CONCLUSION

the very beginnings and boundaries of the universe (if there were indeed boundaries at all), seeking to find that Theory of Everything that would bring together all forces and particles, time and space, in a complete, beautiful package of mathematical understanding.

Understanding Stephen Hawking means understanding how he saw himself. Thankfully, he left us with many exquisitely crafted statements to this effect:

> I am a scientist. And a scientist with a deep fascination with physics, cosmology, the universe and the future of humanity. I was brought up by my parents to have an unwavering curiosity and, like my father, to research and try to answer the many questions that science asks us. I have spent my life travelling across the universe, inside my mind. Through theoretical physics, I have sought to answer some of the great questions. At one point, I thought I would see the end of physics as we know it, but now I think the wonder of discovery will continue long after I am gone. We are close to some of these answers, but we are not there yet.[140]

There is a sense of liberation in this passage, 'unwavering curiosity' leading to cerebral freedom, the open and infinite exploration of reality. He is also excited that scientific exploration will continue long after his earthly existence has ended. In his aforementioned essay 'Will artificial intelligence outsmart us?', Hawking offers a vision of human intelligence defined by the 'ability to adapt to change', this ability refined across thousands of years of evolutionary natural selection. He enjoins us not to fear change, but rather to embrace it. Scientific education is at the heart of this opportunity:

CONCLUSION

> We all have a role to play in making sure that we, and the next generation, have not just the opportunity but the determination to engage fully with the study of science at an early level, so that we can go on to fulfil our potential and create a better world for the whole human race.[141]

We should be careful not to imbue Stephen Hawking with a sainthood he never claimed to possess. In an interview with the *Radio Times* in 2016, Hawking told the interviewer that, 'Just because I spend a lot of time thinking doesn't mean I don't like parties and getting into trouble.'[142] From time to time, scandals and rumours have touched Hawking's reputation.[143] Nor should we give Hawking an oracle-like status, pronouncing the truth on every subject. There were many people who disagreed vehemently with Hawking's arguments, and at times with strong justification. He never won a Nobel Prize, something he seemed to regard with a humorous regret.

Hawking appeared to enjoy his reputation as 'the No 1 celebrity scientist', as Roger Penrose explained in a fond obituary,[144] but Hawking's first love was science. He spent most of his life struggling first-hand with the forces of entropy, gravity and biology, but as long as he could think, then he had the freedom to explore the universe.

BIBLIOGRAPHY

Adler, Jerry, 'Stephen Hawking, Master of the Universe: Our 1988 Cover Story on the Legendary Physicist', *Newsweek* (14 March 2018): https://www.newsweek.com/2018/03/30/stephen-hawking-brief-history-time-oxford-story-844592.html

Bachrach, Judy, 'A Beautiful Mind, an Ugly Possibility', *Vanity Fair* (June 2004): https://www.vanityfair.com/news/2004/06/hawking200406

Boslough, John, *Beyond the Black Hole: Stephen Hawking's Universe* (Glasgow: Fontana/Collins, 1984)

Butler, Isaac, 'Errol Morris on His Movie—and Long Friendship—With Stephen Hawking', *Slate* (16 March 2018): https://slate.com/culture/2018/03/errol-morris-on-stephen-hawking-and-his-movie-a-brief-history-of-time.html

Catholic News Agency, 'Catholics question Hawking's comments on John Paul II' (Washington D.C., 18 June 2006): https://www.catholicnewsagency.com/news/6983/catholics-question-hawkings-comments-on-john-paul-iihttps://www.catholicnewsagency.com/news/6983/catholics-question-hawkings-comments-on-john-paul-ii

CERN, 'Dark Matter': https://home.cern/science/physics/dark-matter, accessed 4 September 2024

Ducharme, Jamie, 'Stephen Hawking Was an Atheist. Here's What He Said About God, Heaven and His Own Death', *Time* (14 March 2018): https://time.com/5199149/stephen-hawking-death-god-atheist/

Ferguson, Kitty, *Stephen Hawking: A Life Well Lived* (London: Penguin, 2019)

Future of Life Institute, 'Research Priorities for Robust and Beneficial Artificial Intelligence: An Open Letter' (2015): https://futureoflife.org/open-letter/ai-open-letter/

Gannon, Megan & LiveScience, 'Stephen Hawking Urges Explorers to Visit Other Planets', Scientific American (18 March 2014): https://www.scientificamerican.com/article/stephen-hawking-urges-explorers-to-visit-other-planets/https://www.scientificamerican.com/article/stephen-hawking-urges-explorers-to-visit-other-planets/

Gleiser, Marcelo, '"Brief Answers To The Big Questions" Is Stephen Hawking's Parting Gift To Humanity', NPR (16 October 2018):

BIBLIOGRAPHY

https://www.npr.org/2018/10/16/657526628/brief-answers-to-the-big-questions-is-stephen-hawkings-parting-gift-to-humanity

Harwood, Michael, 'The Universe and Dr. Hawking', *The New York Times Magazine* (23 January 1983)

Hawking, Jane, *Music to Move the Stars: A Life with Stephen* (London: Pan Books, 2000)

Hawking, Lucy, and Stephen Hawking, *George's Secret Key to the Universe* (London: DoubledDay, 2007); also *George's Cosmic Treasure Hunt* (2009), *George and the Big Bang* (2011), *George and the Unbreakable Code* (2014), *George and the Blue Moon* (2016) and *George and the Ship of Time* (2018)

Hawking, Stephen:

– with George Ellis, 'Singularities in homogeneous world models', *Physics Letters*, 17, 3 (15 July 1965) pp.246–47

– 'Occurrence of Singularities in Open Universes', *Physical Review Letters*, 15, 689 (25 October 1965) p.246

– 'Singularities and the geometry of spacetime' (1966). Republished in *European Physical Journal*, H 39 (2014) pp.413–503

– *Properties of Expanding Universes*, PhD thesis (University of Cambridge: Trinity Hall, 1 February 1966)

– With Roger Penrose, 'On Gravitational Collapse and Cosmology' (1968)

– With George Ellis, 'The Cosmic Black-Body Radiation and the Existence of Singularities in our Universe', *Astrophysical Journal*, 152 (1968) pp.25–36

– With G.W. Gibbons, 'Evidence for black holes in binary star systems', *Nature*, 232 (1971) pp.465–66

– 'Gravitationally Collapsed Objects of Very Low Mass', *Monthly Notices of the Royal Astronomical Society*, Volume 152, Issue 1 (April 1971) pp.75–78

– 'Gravitational Radiation from Colliding Black Holes', *Physics Review Letters*, 26, (24 May 1971) p.1344

– 'The Boundary Conditions of the Universe', *Astrophysical Cosmology; Proceedings of the Study Week on Cosmology and Fundamental Physics* (Vatican City State, 28 September–2 October 1981) pp.563–74

– 'Chronology protection conjecture', *Physics Review*, D 46 (15 July 1992) p.603

BIBLIOGRAPHY

- *Black Holes and Baby Universes and Other Essays* (New York: Bantam, 1993)
- With Roger Penrose, *The Nature of Space and Time* (Princeton, NJ: Princeton University Press, 1996)
- *The Universe in a Nutshell* (London: Bantam Press, 2001)
- *On the Shoulders of Giants: The Great Works of Physics and Astronomy*, ed. with introduction and commentary by Hawking (Philadelphia, PA: Running Press, 2002)
- Ed. with commentary, *God Created the Integers: The Mathematical Breakthroughs That Changed History* (Philadelphia, PA: Running Press, 2005)
- With Leonard Mlodinow, *A Brief History of Time* (London: Bantam, 2005)
- With Thomas Hertog, 'Populating the Landscape: A Top Down Approach', CERN-PH-TH/2006-022 hep-th/0602091 (2006) p.16
- 'Out of a Black Hole', lecture at Caltech (2008)
- With Leonard Mlodinow, *The Grand Design: New Answers to the Ultimate Questions of Life* (London: Transworld, 2010)
- *The Dreams That Stuff Is Made Of: The Most Astounding Papers of Quantum Physics and How They Shook the Scientific World* (Philadelphia, PA: Running Press, 2011)
- *My Brief History* (London: Transworld Publishers, 2013)
- *The Illustrated A Brief History of Time: Updated and Expanded Edition* (London: Transworld Publishers, 2015)
- With Thomas Hertog, 'A smooth exit from eternal inflation?', *Journal of High Energy Physics* (2018) p.147
- *Brief Answers to the Big Questions* (London: John Murray, 2020)

Jamieson, Alastair, 'Stephen Hawking: Donald Trump Appeals to "Lowest Common Denominator"', NBC News (31 May 2016): https://www.nbcnews.com/politics/2016-election/stephen-hawking-donald-trump-appeals-lowest-common-denominator-n583026

Jha, Alok, 'Stephen Hawking: physics would be "more interesting" if Higgs boson hadn't been found', *Guardian* (12 November 2013): https://www.theguardian.com/science/2013/nov/12/stephen-hawking-physics-higgs-boson-particle

Kamberg, Mary-Lane, *Stephen Hawking (Great Science Writers)* (Rosen Young Adult, 2014)

BIBLIOGRAPHY

Jaroff, Leon, 'Stephen Hawking: Roaming the Cosmos', *Time* (8 February 1988): https://content.time.com/time/subscriber/article/0,33009,966650-4,00.html

Penrose, Roger, 'Gravitational Collapse and Space-Time Singularities', *Physical Review Letters*, 14, 3 (January 1965) pp.57–59

Penrose, Roger, '"Mind over matter": Stephen Hawking – obituary by Roger Penrose', *Guardian* (14 March 2018): https://www.theguardian.com/science/2018/mar/14/stephen-hawking-obituary

Petkar, Sofia, 'HAWKING DIES Who is Elaine Mason? Stephen Hawking's ex-wife and nurse was accused of abusing the scientist', *Sun* (15 July 2018): https://www.thesun.co.uk/news/5804564/stephen-hawking-wife-elaine-mason/

Royal Society, 'Hughes Medal': https://royalsociety.org/medals-and-prizes/hughes-medal/, accessed 27 August 2024

Sample, Ian, 'Most threats to humans come from science and technology, warns Hawking', *Guardian* (19 January 2016): https://www.theguardian.com/science/2016/jan/19/stephen-hawking-warns-threats-to-humans-science-technology-bbc-reith-lecture

Sample, Ian, 'Stephen Hawking: 'There is no heaven; it's a fairy story', *Guardian* (15 May 2011): https://www.theguardian.com/science/2011/may/15/stephen-hawking-interview-there-is-no-heaven

Saner, Emine, 'Lucy Hawking's Fears', *Standard* (12 April 2005): https://www.standard.co.uk/showbiz/lucy-hawkings-fears-7232582.html

Smithers, S.R. and R.J. Terry, 'Frank Hawking', Royal College of Physicians: https://history.rcplondon.ac.uk/inspiring-physicians/frank-hawking, accessed 8 September 2024

Susskind, Leonard, *The Black Hole War: Battle with Stephen Hawking to Make the World Safe for Quantum Mechanics* (New York: Little, Brown, 2008)

University of Cambridge, '"The best or worst thing to happen to humanity" – Stephen Hawking launches Centre for the Future of Intelligence' (19 October 2016): https://www.cam.ac.uk/research/news/the-best-or-worst-thing-to-happen-to-humanity-stephen-hawking-launches-centre-for-the-future-of

ENDNOTES

1. Research!America, 'SURVEY: Most Americans Cannot Name a Living Scientist or a Research Institution' (11 May 2021): https://www.researchamerica.org/blog/survey-most-americans-cannot-name-a-living-scientist-or-a-research-institution/

2. Stephen Hawking, *Brief Answers to the Big Questions* (London: Bantam, 2018) p.19

3. Stephen Hawking, *My Brief History* (London: Transworld Publishers, 2013) p.7

4. Ibid., p.17

5. S.R. Smithers and R.J. Terry, 'Frank Hawking', Royal College of Physicians: https://history.rcplondon.ac.uk/inspiring-physicians/frank-hawking

6. Stephen Hawking, 'Professor Stephen Hawking delivers keynote speech on NTDs: YouTube (23 January 2018): https://www.youtube.com/watch?v=ynPOchuVaY8&t=5s

7. Jane Hawking, *Music to Move the Stars: A Life with Stephen* (London: Pan Books, 2000) p.9

8. Hawking, *My Brief History*, p.26

9. Ferguson, Kitty, *Stephen Hawking: A Life Well Lived* (London: Penguin, 2019) p.53

10. Quoted in Mary-Lane Kamberg, *Stephen Hawking (Great Science Writers)* (Rosen Young Adult, 2014)

11. Hawking, *My Brief History*, p.26

12. Ibid., p.35

13. Michael Harwood, 'The Universe and Dr. Hawking', *The New York Times Magazine* (23 January 1983) p.57

14. Stephen Hawking, *The Illustrated A Brief History of Time: Updated and Expanded Edition* (London: Bantam Press, 2015) p.7

15. Ibid., p.9

16. Ibid., p.30

17. Ibid., p.44

18. Ibid., p.235

19. Ibid., p.32

20. Ibid., p.34

21. Stephen Hawking, *Brief Answers to the Big Questions* (London: John Murray, 2020) p.94

22. Ibid., p.95

23. Ibid., p.9

24. Hawking, *Brief History*, p.50

25. Ibid., p.106

26. Ibid., p.105

27. Ibid., p.109

28. Ibid., p.110

29. Hawking, *My Brief History*, p.47

30. John Boslough, *Beyond the Black Hole: Stephen Hawking's Universe* (Glasgow: Fontana/Collins, 1984) p.107

31. Hawking, *My Brief History*, p.122

32. Ferguson, *Stephen Hawking*, p.72

33. Jane Hawking. *Travelling to Infinity: My Life with Stephen* (London: Alma Books, 2010) p.14

34. Ibid., p.18

35. Ibid., p.20

36. Ibid., p.25

37. Ferguson, *Stephen Hawking*, p.79

38. Hawking, *My Brief History*, p.61

39. See Roger Penrose, 'Gravitational Collapse and Space-Time Singularities', *Physical Review Letters*, 14, 3 (January 1965) pp.57–59

40. Stephen Hawking and George Ellis, 'Singularities in homogeneous world models', *Physics Letters*, 17, 3 (15 July 1965) pp.246–47

ENDNOTES

41. Stephen Hawking, 'Occurrence of Singularities in Open Universes', *Physical Review Letters*, 15, 689 (25 October 1965) p.246

42. Hawking, *My Brief History*, p.64

43. Ibid.

44. S.W. Hawking, *Properties of Expanding Universes*, PhD thesis (University of Cambridge: Trinity Hall, 1 February 1966) p.2

45. Stephen Hawking, *The Universe in a Nutshell* (London: Bantam Press, 2001) p.41

46. Stephen Hawking, 'Singularities and the geometry of spacetime' (1966). Republished in *European Physical Journal*, H 39 (2014) pp.413–503

47. Ibid.

48. Stephen Hawking and Roger Penrose, 'On Gravitational Collapse and Cosmology' (1968)

49. Stephen Hawking and George Ellis, 'The Cosmic Black-Body Radiation and the Existence of Singularities in our Universe', *Astrophysical Journal*, 152 (1968) pp.25–36

50. Hawking, *Brief History of Time*, p.156

51. Ibid., p.60

52. Jane Hawking, *Travelling to Infinity*, p.57

53. Hawking, *Brief History of Time*, p.111

54. Hawking, *My Brief History*, p.69

55. Stephen Hawking, 'Gravitational Radiation from Colliding Black Holes', *Physics Review Letters*, 26, (24 May 1971) p.1344

56. Ferguson, *Stephen Hawking*, p.320

57. Stephen Hawking, 'Gravitationally Collapsed Objects of Very Low Mass', *Monthly Notices of the Royal Astronomical Society*, Volume 152, Issue 1 (April 1971) pp.75–78

58. Hawking, *Brief History of Time*, p.132

59. Hawking, *Nutshell*, p.118

60. Ibid.

61. Alexis Lutz, 'Doctor Stephen Hawking in 1977', BBC, YouTube: https://www.youtube.com/watch?v=RBhTGf9Bov4

62. Jane Hawking, *Travelling to Infinity*, p.216

63. Hawking, *Brief History of Time*, p.245

64. Ferguson, *Stephen Hawking*, p.174

65. Stephen Hawking, 'Out of a Black Hole', lecture at Caltech (2008)

66. Leonard Susskind, *The Black Hole War: My Battle with Stephen Hawking to Make the World Safe for Quantum Mechanics* (New York: Little, Brown, 2008)

67. Jane Hawking, *Travelling to Infinity*, p.285

68. Hawking, *My Brief History*, p.85

69. Royal Society, 'Hughes Medal': https://royalsociety.org/medals-and-prizes/hughes-medal/, accessed 27 August 2024

70. Hawking, *Brief History of Time*, p.88

71. Ibid.

72. Alok Jha, 'Stephen Hawking: physics would be "more interesting" if Higgs boson hadn't been found', *Guardian* (12 November 2013): https://www.theguardian.com/science/2013/nov/12/stephen-hawking-physics-higgs-boson-particle

73. Ibid.

74. Boslough, *Beyond the Black Hole*, p.100

75. Hawking, *Brief History*, p.214

76. Jane Hawking, *Travelling to Infinity*, p.178

77. Stephen Hawking, 'The Boundary Conditions of the Universe.' *Astrophysical Cosmology; Proceedings of the Study Week on Cosmology and Fundamental Physics* (Vatican City State, 28 September–2 October 1981) pp.563–574.

78. Hawking, *Universe in a Nutshell*, p.59

79. Ibid., p.80

80. Ibid., p.85

81. Hawking, *Brief History of Time*, p.138

82. Catholic News Agency, 'Catholics question Hawking's comments on John Paul II'

ENDNOTES

(Washington D.C., 18 June 2006): https://www.catholicnewsagency.com/news/6983/catholics-question-hawkings-comments-on-john-paul-ii

83. Royal Society, 'Stephen Hawking'

84. Hawking, *My Brief History*, p.87

85. Ibid., p.92

86. Ferguson, *Stephen Hawking*, p.231

87. Leon Jaroff, 'Stephen Hawking: Roaming the Cosmos', Time (8 February 1988): https://content.time.com/time/subscriber/article/0,33009,966650-4,00.html

88. Ibid.

89. Hawking, *My Brief History*, p.98

90. Marcelo Gleiser, '"Brief Answers To The Big Questions" Is Stephen Hawking's Parting Gift To Humanity', NPR (16 October 2018): https://www.npr.org/2018/10/16/657526628/brief-answers-to-the-big-questions-is-stephen-hawkings-parting-gift-to-humanity

91. Jerry Adler, 'Stephen Hawking, Master of the Universe: Our 1988 Cover Story on the Legendary Physicist', Newsweek (14 March 2018): https://www.newsweek.com/2018/03/30/stephen-hawking-brief-history-time-oxford-story-844592.html

92. Hawking, *Brief History of Time*, p.203

93. Ibid., p.205

94. Ibid., p.210. Also Stephen Hawking, 'Chronology protection conjecture', *Physics Review*, D 46 (15 July 1992) p.603

95. Hawking, *Universe in a Nutshell*, p.148

96. Hawking, *Brief History of Time*, p.210

97. Ferguson, *Stephen Hawking*, p.298

98. Hawking, *Brief History of Time*, p.210

99. Ibid., p.211

100. Ibid., p.216

101. Ibid.

102. Ibid., pp.216–17

103. Hawking, *Universe in a Nutshell*, p.54

104. Ibid., p.175

105. Ibid., p.184

106. CERN, 'Dark Matter': https://home.cern/science/physics/dark-matter, accessed 4 September 2024

107. Ibid., p.198

108. Hawking, *My Brief History*, p.87

109. Ferguson, *Stephen Hawking*, p.279

110. Isaac Butler, 'Errol Morris on His Movie—and Long Friendship—With Stephen Hawking', *Slate* (16 March 2018): https://slate.com/culture/2018/03/errol-morris-on-stephen-hawking-and-his-movie-a-brief-history-of-time.html

111. Ibid.

112. Quoted in Bob Sipchen, 'Simply Human: Science: Wheelchair-bound physicist Stephen Hawking resists efforts to deify his life or his disabilities', *Los Angeles Times* (6 June 1990: https://www.latimes.com/archives/la-xpm-1990-06-06-vw-538-story.html

113. Hawking, *My Brief History*, p.91

114. Emine Saner, 'Lucy Hawking's Fears', *Standard* (12 April 2005): https://www.standard.co.uk/showbiz/lucy-hawkings-fears-7232582.html

115. Judy Bachrach, 'A Beautiful Mind, an Ugly Possibility', *Vanity Fair* (June 2004): https://www.vanityfair.com/news/2004/06/hawking200406

116. Sofia Petkar, 'HAWKING DIES Who is Elaine Mason? Stephen Hawking's ex-wife and nurse was accused of abusing the scientist', *Sun* (15 July 2018): https://www.thesun.co.uk/news/5804564/stephen-hawking-wife-elaine-mason/

117. Hawking, *My Brief History*, p.89

118. Stephen Hawking and Thomas Hertog, 'Populating the Landscape: A Top Down Approach', CERN-PH-TH/2006-022 hep-th/0602091 (2006) p.16

ENDNOTES

119. Ibid., p.18

120. Stephen Hawking and Thomas Hertog, 'A smooth exit from eternal inflation?', *Journal of High Energy Physics* (2018) p.147

121. Hawking, *The Grand Design*, p.8

122. Ibid., p.7

123. Ibid., p.51

124. Ibid., p.5

125. Ibid., p.8

126. Hawking, *Brief Answers to the Big Questions*, p.38

127. Ian Sample, 'Stephen Hawking: 'There is no heaven; it's a fairy story', *Guardian* (15 May 2011): https://www.theguardian.com/science/2011/may/15/stephen-hawking-interview-there-is-no-heaven

128. Jamie Ducharme, 'Stephen Hawking Was an Atheist. Here's What He Said About God, Heaven and His Own Death', *Time* (14 March 2018): https://time.com/5199149/stephen-hawking-death-god-atheist/

129. Alastair Jamieson, Stephen Hawking: Donald Trump Appeals to "Lowest Common Denominator", NBC News (31 May 2016): https://www.nbcnews.com/politics/2016-election/stephen-hawking-donald-trump-appeals-lowest-common-denominator-n583026

130. Stephen Hawking, Speech at 2012 London Paralympics (29 August 2012)

131. Hawking, *Brief Answers to the Big Questions*, p.187

132. Future of Life Institute, 'Research Priorities for Robust and Beneficial Artificial Intelligence: An Open Letter' (2015): https://futureoflife.org/open-letter/ai-open-letter/

133. University of Cambridge, '"The best or worst thing to happen to humanity" – Stephen Hawking launches Centre for the Future of Intelligence' (19 October 2016): https://www.cam.ac.uk/research/news/the-best-or-worst-thing-to-happen-to-humanity-stephen-hawking-launches-centre-for-the-future-of

134. Hawking, *Brief Answers*, p.134

135. Ibid., p.81

136. Ibid., p.80

137. Ibid., p.169

138. Megan Gannon & LiveScience, 'Stephen Hawking Urges Explorers to Visit Other Planets', Scientific American (18 March 2014): https://www.scientificamerican.com/article/stephen-hawking-urges-explorers-to-visit-other-planets/

139. Hawking, *Brief Answers*, p.144

140. Hawking, *Brief Answers*, pp.4–5

141. Ibid., p.195

142. Ian Sample, 'Most threats to humans come from science and technology, warns Hawking', *Guardian* (19 January 2016): https://www.theguardian.com/science/2016/jan/19/stephen-hawking-warns-threats-to-humans-science-technology-bbc-reith-lecture

143. Some of the most suggestive allegations about Hawking came in 2024. In March 2006, Hawking and a group of other esteemed scientists attended a conference on gravity on the private island of Little Saint James in the Caribbean. The island was owned, and the conference arranged by, the now infamous sex offender Jeffrey Epstein, although no wrongdoing has been imputed to Hawking or any of the other scientists who attended.

144. Roger Penrose, '"Mind over matter": Stephen Hawking – obituary by Roger Penrose', *Guardian* (14 March 2018): https://www.theguardian.com/science/2018/mar/14/stephen-hawking-obituary

INDEX

Adams, Douglas 162
Adams, John Couch 78
Adams Prize 78–9
Ampère, André-Marie 37
anthropic principle 118–19
arrow of time 121–2
Artificial Intelligence (AI) 183–5
Aventis Prizes for Science Books 131

Bekenstein, Jacob 93, 95
Benjamin Franklin Medal in Physics 121
Big Bang theory 57, 63, 80, 81, 99, 113–14, 115
Big Crunch theory 81, 150
black holes 57–61, 87–99, 147, 170–1
Black Holes and Baby Universes and Other Essays (Hawking) 131, 140
Blackburn, Sam 168
Bohr, Niels 32
Boslough, John 65, 114
bosons 47–8, 111–12
'Boundary Conditions of the Universe, The' (Hawking) 115–19
brane worlds 148–9, 150
Brave New World with Stephen Hawking (TV series) 163
Breakthrough Starshot project 187–8
Brief Answers to the Big Questions (Hawking) 53, 133–4, 177
Brief History of Time, A (film) 154–6

Brief History of Time, A (Hawking)
on Albert Einstein 42
on black holes 58, 59, 89, 93
on CMBR 80
on cosmology 56
on electrodynamics 37–8
on entropy 40–1
on general relativity 42, 47
on inflationary universe 80
on Newtonian physics 34, 35–6
for popular audience 33
publication of 125–31
on quantum mechanics 51
on quarks 47
on religion
on special relativity 42, 45–6
on string theory 144
on *Theory of Everything* 110, 114
on time travel 141, 144
on wormholes 137–8, 139
Brief History of Time, A: A Reader's Companion 156
Briefer History of Time, A (Hawking & Mlodinow) 132
Bucher, Martin 150
Byron House School 15

California Institute of Technology (Caltech) 88, 99–104
Cambridge University 31–3, 63, 70–82, 83, 106–7, 108–9
'Can we predict the future?' (Hawking) 51
Carr, Bernard 100–1
Carter, Brandon 73, 94
Cartwright, Nancy 131
Casimir effect 139
Catholic News Agency 119
Cauchy, Augustin-Louis 75
Cauchy surface 75–6
Chadwick, James 46
Chandrasekhar, Subrahmanyan 59
Chomsky, Noam 178
classical physics
electrodynamics 37–9
Newtonian physics 33–7
thermodynamics 39–41
climate change 182
Clinton, Bill 160
colonization of space 180–1, 186–8
Compton, Arthur H. 43
'Cosmic Black-Body Radiation and the Existence of Singularities in our Universe' (Ellis & Hawking) 79
cosmic censorship hypothesis 90–1
cosmic microwave background radiation (CMBR) 57, 72, 79–80, 143
cosmology 54–7

203

INDEX

Cox, Brian 158
Cumberbatch, Benedict 153–4, 163
dark matter 149–52

Denman, Pete 168
Dicke, Robert 57
Dirac, Paul 32, 102
Donovan, Robert 66
Doppler, Christian 56
Dreams That Stuff Is Made of, The: The Most Astounding Papers of Quantum Physics and How They Shook the Scientific World (Hawking) 132–3

Eddington, Arthur 50
Einstein, Albert 32, 39
  and cosmology 54–5, 56
  and general relativity 46, 48–51
  and quantum mechanics 53
  and special relativity 42–3, 45–6
  and wormholes 138
Einstein–Rosen bridge 138
El Mundo 177
Elder, John 28
electrodynamics 37–9
Ellis, George 66, 72, 74, 125
Englert, François 112
entropy 40–1, 93–4, 121–2
Equalizer (speech to text technology) 123–4, 155
European Organization for Nuclear Research (CERN) 112, 122, 149
Evans, Lucille 123
event horizon 60, 87–91, 93–6
'Evidence for black holes in binary star systems' (Gibbons & Hawking) 88

Faraday, Michael 32, 37
Fella, Judy 107
Ferguson, Kitty 84, 105, 152
Fermi, Enrico 32
Ferris, Timothy 132
Feynman, Richard 101, 117
Finkelstein, David 60
Franklin Institute 121
Freedman, Gordon 154–5
Friedmann, Alex 55, 80
Friedmann-Robertson-Walker (FRW) model 74
Future of Life Institute 184
Future of Spacetime, The (Ferris, Hawking, Novikov & Thorne) 132

Galfard, Christophe 132, 163
Galileo 13, 32, 102
Gell-Mann, Murray 101
general relativity 46–51
genetic engineering 185
George, Danielle 163
George's Secret Key to the Universe series (Galfard, Hawking & Hawking) 85, 132
Geroch, Robert 76
Gibbons, Gary 88
Glass, Philip 155
Gleiser, Marcelo 134
God Created the Integers: The Mathematical Breakthroughs That Changed History 132
Goldhaber, Alfred 150
Grand Design, The: New Answers to the Ultimate Questions of Life (Hawking & Mlodinow) 132, 172–6
Grand Unified Theory (GUT) 109 see also Theory of Everything
Graves, Beryl 19

Graves, Robert 19
Graves, William 19–20
'Gravitational Radiation from Colliding Black Holes' (Hawking) 90
'Gravitationally Collapsed Objects of Very Low Mass' (Hawking) 92
Guardian, The 177
Guth, Alan 120
Guzzardi, Peter 127

Hartle, Jim 101, 118
Hartle–Hawking wave function 117
Harvard University 160
Haussecker, Horst 168
Hawking (film) 153–4
Hawking, Edward (brother) 14
Hawking, Frank (father) 11–13, 14, 15–19, 23, 24, 64, 70, 156
Hawking, Isobel (mother) 12–13, 14–15, 16, 19, 64, 156
Hawking, Jane (wife) 19
  and *A Brief History of Time* film 156
  birth of children 84–5
  at Caltech 100
  career sacrifices 85–6, 100
  early relationship with Stephen Hawking 67–70
  family life 98–9
  and Jonathan Hellyer Jones 107–8, 152–3
  later career of 153–4
  marriage to Stephen Hawking 82–3, 114, 152–3
  during pneumonia bout 122
  religious beliefs 114

204

INDEX

Hawking, Lucy (daughter) 85, 125–6, 132, 134, 165–6, 167
Hawking, Mary (grandmother) 12
Hawking, Mary (sister) 14
Hawking, Phillipa (sister) 14
Hawking, Robert (grandfather) 12
Hawking, Robert (son) 84–5, 86, 99
Hawking, Stephen
  and Artificial Intelligence 183–5
  as author 124–34
  birth of 13–14
  birth of children 84–5
  at Caltech 99–104
  CBE for 121
  celebrity status 121, 134–5, 140–1, 154–65
  childhood of 14–15, 16, 18–20
  and climate change 182
  and colonization of space 180–1, 186–8
  communication technology for 123–4, 167–9
  continued visits to United States 104–5
  death of 188–9
  diagnosis of motor neuron disease 64–6
  and disability rights 159, 179
  early press appearances 98–9
  and Elaine Mason 152–3, 156, 165–7
  family life 98–9
  as Fellow of the Royal Society (FRS) 97–8
  first signs of motor neuron disease 29–30, 32
  and genetic engineering 185
  honorary doctorate from Harvard University 160
  international reputation of 101–2
  in Iran 28–9
  legacy of 7–8
  as Lucasian Chair of Mathematics 108–9
  marriage to Jane Hawking 82–3, 152–3
  and nuclear weapons 182–3
  OBE for 134
  with pneumonia 122–3
  political views of 178–80
  postgraduate research at Cambridge University 31–3, 63, 70–82
  readership post at Cambridge University 106–7
  relationship with Jane Wilde 67–70
  research fellowship at Cambridge University 82, 83
  religious beliefs 113–19, 172–6
  and Roman Catholic Church 113–19
  at St Albans School 20–1, 22–3
  teenage years 21–2
  as undergraduate at Oxford University 22–8
  worsening symptoms of motor neuron disease 83–4
Hawking radiation 92–7, 101, 104, 120, 170
Heisenberg, Werner 32, 52
Heisenberg's uncertainty principle 52–3, 94, 95–6

Hellyer Jones, Jonathan 107–8, 152–3
Hertog, Thomas 169, 171–2
Hickman, David 155
Higgs, Peter 111, 112
Higgs boson 111–12
Hitchhiker's Guide to the Galaxy, The (Adams) 162
holographic principle 147–9, 171
Hooft, Gerard 't 147
Hoyle, Fred 57, 63, 71–2, 84
Hubble, Edwin 55–6
Hughes Medal 108
Humphrey, John 24
Hunt, Jeremy 179
'Imagination and Change: Science in the Next Millennium' (Hawking) 160
inflationary universe 80–2, 119–21, 150–1, 171–2
information paradox 103–4, 105, 147, 170–1
Into the Universe with Stephen Hawking (TV documentary) 140–1, 163

Iran 28–9

Jaded (Hawking) 165
Jones, Felicity 164–5

Kane, Gordon 111
Kepler, Johannes 32
Key to the Universe, The (TV documentary) 98–9
Khalatnikov, Isaak 73

Laflamme, Raymond 121, 122
Laplace, Pierre-Simon 32, 53
Large Hadron Collider (LHC) 111–12

INDEX

Large Scale Structure of Space-Time, The (Ellis & Hawking) 125
Large, The, the Small and the Human Mind (Cartwright, Hawking & Shimony) 131
Lemaître, Georges 55, 57
Leverhulme Centre for the Future of Intelligence (CFI) 184
Lifshitz, Evgeny 73
Lightman, Alan 132
Linde, Andrei 120, 171–2
'Logical Uniselector Computing Engine' (LUCE) 2

M-theory 146–7, 174
MacArthur Foundation 123
Maldacena, Juan Martín 170–1
Martin, Philip 153
Mason, David 124, 152–3
Mason, Elaine 123, 152–3, 156, 165–7
Master of the Universe (TV documentary) 135
Maxwell, James Clerk 32, 37–8
McCarten, Anthony 164
Michell, John 59
Michelson, Albert 39
Michelson–Morley experiment 39
Millikan, Robert 43
Milner, Yuri 187
Mlodinow, Leonard 132, 172, 175, 176
model-dependent realism 174–6
Moffat, Peter 153
Morley, Edward 39
Morris, Errol 155, 156

Music to Move the Stars: A Life with Stephen (Hawking) 153
Musk, Elon 186–7
My Brief History (Hawking) 14, 15, 130, 133, 167

Nachman, Lama 168
Nambu, Yoichiro 143
Narlikar, Jayant 71
National Institute for Medical Research 15, 17
Nature of Space and Time, The (Hawking & Penrose) 131
Newman, David 178
Newsweek (magazine) 134–5
Newton, Isaac 32, 33–7, 98
Newtonian physics 33–7
Nielsen, Holger Bech 143
Nimoy, Leonard 157
no-boundary condition 115–19
no-boundary multiverse model 169–70
Novikov, Igor 132
nuclear weapons 182–3

'Occurrence of Singularities in Open Universes' (Hawking) 75
'On the Electrodynamics of Moving Bodies' (Einstein) 43
'On Gravitational Collapse and Cosmology' (Hawking & Penrose) 78–9
On the Shoulders of Giants: The Great Works of Physics and Astronomy 132
Oppenheimer, J. Robert 59–60

Oxford University 22–8

Page, Don 101, 105, 107, 121, 128
Paralympic Games (2012) 179
pea instanton theory 150–2
Penrose, Roger 57, 72–3, 74–5, 77, 78–9, 87, 90, 131, 194
Penzias, Arno 57
Perry, Malcolm 171
Philosophiæ Naturalis Principia Mathematica (Mathematical Principles of Natural Philosophy) (Newton) 34–5
Planck, Max 32, 43, 52
Pontifical Academy of Sciences 102, 113
Pope Pius VI Medal 102, 113
'Populating the Landscape: A Top Down Approach' (Hawking & Hertog) 169–70
Powney, Derek 27
Preskill, John 91, 171

quantum mechanics 51–3, 94–5
quarks 47

Radio Times 194
Redmayne, Eddie 134, 164–5
Rees, Martin 66
Research!America 8
Robertson, Howard P. 80–1
Roemer, Ole 43, 59
Roman Catholic Church 113–19
Rosen, Nathan 138
Royal Society (FRS) 97–8
Rutherford–Chadwick model 46–7

INDEX

Rutherford, Ernest 46

Sagan, Carl 129
St Albans High School for Girls 19
St Albans School 20–1, 22–3
Saner, Emine 165, 167
Schrödinger, Erwin 32, 52
Sciama, Dennis 63, 70, 84
Shatner, William 162
Search for a New Earth, The (TV documentary) 163
Shimony, Abner 131
Sightsavers 17–18
Simpsons, The 158
singularities 57, 72–9
'Singularities and the geometry of spacetime' (Hawking) 77–8
'Singularities in homogeneous world models' (Ellis & Hawking) 74
Sitter, Willem de 55
'Smooth Exit from Eternal Inflation, A' (Hawking & Hertog) 171–2
Snyder, Hartland 60
special relativity 42–6
Spielberg, Steven 155, 156
Standard Model 109, 111
Star Trek: The Next Generation 157–8
Starobinsky, Alexander 94, 95
steady-state theory 56–7, 63
Stephen Hawking's Favorite Places (TV documentary) 163
Stephen Hawking's Universe (TV documentary) 140–1, 162–3
string theory 143–7

Strominger, Andrew 171
Sulphonamides, The (Hawking) 17
sum-over-histories approach 117–18
superstring theory 145–6
supersymmetry model 111, 145
Susskind, Leonard 143, 147, 171

Tahta, Dikran 22–3
Taylor, John G. 97
Theory of Everything, The 109–12, 114, 143, 146–7, 148
Theory of Everything, The (film) 164–5
thermodynamics 39–41
Thomson, J.J. 47
Thorne, Kip 89, 91, 100, 101, 132, 134, 171
Time (magazine) 128, 131
time travel 140–3
Travelling to Infinity: The True Story Behind the Theory of Everything (Hawking) 153, 164
Trump, Donald 178
Truth is in the Stars, The (TV documentary) 162
Turok, Neil 150, 151

Universe in a Nutshell, The (Hawking) 77, 131, 143–4, 146, 147, 148, 150

Vanity Fair (magazine) 166
Veneziano, Gabriele 143

Walker, Arthur 80–1
Wheeler, John 59, 88
White House Millennium Lecture Series 160
Whitt, Brian 127

Wilde, Jane
 see Hawking, Jane
Wilson, Robert 57
Witten, Edward 147
Woltosz, Ginger 123
Woltosz, Walter (Walt) 123
wormholes 137–40

Zeldovich, Yakov 94, 95
Zuckerberg, Mark 187
Zuckerman, Al 126

207

PICTURE CREDITS

10 Alamy Stock Photo/Tom Pilston
14 Alamy Stock Photo/ Archivio GBB
26 Alamy Stock Photo/Krzysztof Jakubczyk
29 Alamy Stock Photo/Peregrine
31 Alamy Stock Photo/Album
60 Alamy Stock Photo/Krzysztof Jakubczyk
61 Alamy Stock Photo/Krzysztof Jakubczyk
67 Alamy Stock Photo/Ian Dagnall Computing
108 Alamy Stock Photo/Liam White
129 Alamy Stock Photo/Art Directors & TRIP/Helen Rogers
133 Alamy Stock Photo/Miguel Sayago
151 Alamy Stock Photo/PA Images/Michael Stephens
157 Alamy Stock Photo/ Paramount/Courtesy Everett Collection
160 Alamy Stock Photo/Miguel Sayago
164 Alamy Stock Photo/ NASA Photo
166 Alamy Stock Photo/Stills Press
180 Alamy Stock Photo/White House Photo
189 Alamy Stock Photo/PA Images/Joe Giddens
192 Alamy Stock Photo/Geopix